NO GREATER LOVE

No Greater Love

JOY BATH
WITH SHIRLEY COLLINS

KINGSWAY PUBLICATIONS
EASTBOURNE

First published 1995
Reprinted 1996

ISBN 0 85476 578 6

Designed and produced by
Bookprint Creative Services
P.O. Box 827, BN21 3YJ, England for
KINGSWAY PUBLICATIONS LTD
Lottbridge Drove, Eastbourne, E. Sussex BN23 6NT.
Printed in Great Britain.

Foreword

It is never easy to give an answer to the age-old question, 'How does a loving God allow suffering?' It is sometimes even harder to understand why, when someone serves God all their life, suffering follows. *No Greater Love* confesses that it does not try to give slick answers to either of these questions, but it does continually show that despite the hardships and testings of Joy Bath, plus many other characters mentioned in her memoirs, God is always to be trusted. A peace that passes all understanding fills our hearts when we put ourselves into the hands of the Almighty, no matter what happens to us.

Roy Castle
Spring 1994

Introduction

How can one person judge the life of another? It was a privilege to ghost-write this book for Joy. I make no pretence of being the same kind of selfless person she was. She gave her time sacrificially, and I have undoubtedly spent more of my time on earth enjoying myself. We could work together because we were both travelling the same road: we shared the same Christian faith.

In my walk with God I have been impressed by the work of the Reverend Malcolm Herbert. Two decades ago he and I attended the same youth group. Now he is a vicar, currently in Woking. He has spoken these words of wisdom which are relevant to society, and to how it may regard people such as Joy; people the world may consider insignificant: 'We live in a society which majors on success and despises failure. But the world is groaning like a woman in labour. And us with it. We are simultaneously part of the problem and the answer. We are not called to succeed, but to follow Jesus.'

Joy was not a natural writer. Her diaries contained mundane things like, 'Washed my hair. Did the washing up before lights out.' Mixed in with these comments were simple statements such as, 'Helped with a Caesarean section.' She did not boast of her achievements; would not mention how the lives of thousands of patients had been saved through the medical knowledge of herself and her colleagues. To discover the stories behind her daily jottings it was necessary to sit alongside Joy and talk at length. Drawing out the facts from such a retiring and phlegmatic individual was not easy. In the process I discovered a modern-day saint with a terrific sense of humour.

I also spoke to a number of friends, colleagues and members of the Bath family, who provided additional insights into Joy's life. The Bishop of Salisbury told me: 'In the end, when you meet death face to face, there is nothing else in which to put your trust except God.'

Joy Bath trusted God—in life and in death.

Shirley Collins

I

'It won't work! This jack—it doesn't fit our wheels, Joy.'

I watched, helpless, as Debbie Brown, my nursing Sister, tried to lift the pick-up to change a punctured tyre. Too ill to be of much practical help, I felt anxious about our predicament on a dirt road in the middle of nowhere.

The sun rose higher, along with my temperature and Debbie's temper. We were both red in the face when I suggested she ought to stop for a cool drink. In her best Irish brogue she told me to push off—to go and sit under the shade of the nearest bush. I watched my colleague from a distance. Of medium height, slim build and with a fair complexion, we are very much alike: both lacking in muscle power and unsuited to an African heatwave.

It was Sunday 8th March 1992. The weather had been extremely hot almost since the year began, when the rains failed to come. Zimbabwe's worst drought in living memory marked the start of a different kind of aridity in my own life. We were on our way to Harare, setting off early to avoid the intolerable heat of the day. The Elim Mission Hospital truck was due for a service, and I was hoping to find a cure for a prolonged fever, nasty cough, sore throat and various aches and pains which refused to respond to antibiotics. Poorly on and off for about a year, the symptoms had escalated over the previous month until my chest hurt just in breathing.

Debbie persevered for well over an hour. When people

get angry, they somehow gain extra strength. In her frustration she found a way to make the jack stay on the wheel. Slowly, inch by inch, one corner of the truck was raised off the ground. The job was three-quarters done when I spotted an approaching bus. It stopped and all the passengers piled out, eager to help.

'You know, I'm actually annoyed those guys arrived after I'd done the hardest part,' Debbie frowned, as the journey recommenced.

'You should demand a discount from the garage. Part of the service has been done already!' Realising the humour of the situation we laughed, relieved to be *en route* once more.

Arriving in Harare around midday, exhausted, grubby and dishevelled, all I could manage was to shower and collapse into bed. Thankfully we were at the home of senior Elim mission workers Peter and Brenda Griffiths; old friends who were not expecting me to provide scintillating conversation over lunch.

Next morning I was well enough to visit the local doctor's surgery for a thorough examination, and go for blood and urine tests. More antibiotics were prescribed—this time for pus on the tonsils. Though I had no idea I could be a risk to anyone, I remember commenting that the young lady who took the blood sample should have been wearing rubber gloves.

Three days passed with Peter and Brenda. The cough and chest pain became much worse so the local doctor advised admission to hospital. An empty bed was found in St Anne's, Harare. While Peter rummaged through Brenda's shelves for a suitable nightdress and dressing gown for me to borrow, I rang my parents in England. About to leave for a holiday in Spain, they sounded really concerned and considered cancelling. Thinking they were overreacting, I persuaded them to go ahead as planned.

Back at the Mission prayers were said for me. Dr Roger

Drew, who gave treatment in the early stages, kept in touch with Peter by telephone. Tuberculosis or typhoid might account for my problems. When pneumonia was diagnosed, Roger became alarmed. He needed to visit Harare to buy some electrical equipment so hc decided to check on me at the same time.

One morning, as a nurse helped me to bathe, I commented on my sudden weight loss. Two-thirds of the patients I cared for as Matron of the seventy-bed Mission hospital had AIDS. I had begun to look like one of them. The nurse made no reply, but must have said something to the consultant as he came to me requesting an AIDS test.

'It really isn't necessary,' I replied. 'During a visit home in 1990 I had a test, which was negative.'

'You could have become infected since then.'

'We've been careful to wear rubber gloves at work, sterilising them with bleach before re-using. There's been no unprotected exposure.' I thought of my young niece back in England, who organised a glove collection as a safeguard against AIDS infection.

'I'm afraid I must insist you take another test now,' he said firmly.

I had faith in Dr Wiles, and submitted. At least I would be able to prove him wrong.

My rough breathing disturbed some of the other patients. Moved to a side ward, I waited with Roger on Saturday 21st March for the results of the blood test for AIDS. For me there was no stomach sickening anxiety, as I was confident the result would be negative, even though the evidence was ominous. Roger had looked at my latest chest X-ray. It was very abnormal, and an accompanying report raised the possibility of sarcoidosis—a fleshy tumour. But why should someone like me, a non-smoker, develop such a thing?

Whatever the cause, my condition would soon begin to

improve, I told myself, and before long I would return to the demanding job I enjoyed so much. It was not to be. I was unaware that Roger already knew the worst. Informed the day before, he had been trying to prepare me to face the truth. Now Consultant Dr Wiles was coming towards us, the gravity of his expression warning that something was wrong. He looked down at the floor for an instant, hesitated, then looked me straight in the eye. 'You've tested HIV-positive.'

'I can't be,' I protested and demanded a retest, adding, 'I don't remember any needle-stick injuries. It must be a mistake.'

'I'm sorry,' he said, leaving me to come to terms with the shock and feelings of disbelief.

Peter Griffiths entered at that moment. It was quite early in the morning, but he had been waiting in the foyer at Roger's request. The three of us sat and wept together for ages. When Dr Wiles returned he said something of great significance, although it gave little comfort at the time.

'For you, Joy, the fact that you are HIV-positive is not a matter for shame, but for pride.'

'Yes,' said Peter. 'You have the virus only because of your calling and dedication to service.'

'You must realise you are seriously ill, and it's best that you return to England as soon as possible,' continued Dr Wiles.

'I'll make the necessary arrangements,' volunteered Roger.

'And I'll go back to Katerere with Roger and tell everyone at the Mission,' said Peter, ever the calm organiser, though he looked shaken.

Roger had a real battle to get me on a plane to Heathrow. Very politely he was told to delay travel until his patient was feeling better. Only when he spoke to the British Airways doctor in London, fully explaining the situation, did things begin to move. In the meantime I really appreciated the visit of a contingent from the Mission around my bedside. Emotions were running riot as we said our goodbyes. No one knew what to say; no words seemed adequate. Pastor Munembe was there, Mai Simango—who had worked closely with me in the Sunday school—all the national nurses, and Debbie.

After the others had gone Debbie stayed behind. Now she was telling me of her long-standing fears that I might have AIDS. Though I knew I would never work in Africa again, the full implications of my physical state had not yet struck home. As far as I was concerned I had contracted the HIV virus and developed pneumonia as a result. The fact that Debbie was talking about AIDS didn't register in my mind. That was one more hurdle yet to be faced.

Three days later, strapped to a stretcher and with an oxygen mask over my face, I made the ambulance ride from St Anne's to Harare Airport. Peter and Debbie were also in attendance, together with Roger, who was travelling with me. It must have looked a fearful scene to other passengers—like something from a television soap—but this was real-life drama. Some doubted I would survive the long journey. They were praying hard that life would still be present by touchdown and beyond, to Southampton General Hospital.

I slept most of the way while Roger watched the in-flight movie, *Terminator 2: Judgement Day.* Charity and mission workers normally take the cheapest seats. Due to my state of health we travelled First Class. Roger joked that he would be returning as baggage. Thanks to his diplomacy, no one on the plane or at Elim Headquarters was aware of the full story of my condition. I wanted my parents to be the next to know, and I wanted to be the person to tell them. When we were able to talk together their reaction was strange, as if my words were fulfilling some kind of prophecy.

'We feel the Lord has prepared us for this. We're not at all surprised,' said Mum. At that moment all I wanted was for them to put their arms around me and hold me tight. I found out later that that was what they wanted too, but at the time it was difficult—I had tubes everywhere, and they didn't want me to break down and cry in case it restricted my breathing even further.

I arrived in England at the time of the Elim Pentecostal Church's annual conference, which was being held at Butlin's, Bognor Regis. Many members were following my career with interest. When those at the conference heard the latest news, which Roger had drafted into an official statement, 4,000 people rose from their seats, joined hands and prayed for me. I believe those prayers had an effect. After responding to treatment for pneumocystis pneumonia (PCP) I was well enough, a few days later, to address the conference via a live telephone link. The nurses were left wondering whether their patient was a new celebrity.

I began to feel more comfortable. Then, about three weeks after the initial diagnosis, the reality of my illness began to sink in. I had attended AIDS courses and nursed AIDS patients for four years. Only now did it dawn on me that PCP plus HIV-positive equals full-blown AIDS; a death sentence. Coming from a pentecostal background I automatically began asking God for healing, and questioned how I could have contracted the disease.

I still have no idea how it happened. There are theories about bleach weakening the protection of surgical gloves, and stories of medics becoming infected through body fluids splashing in the eyes. Or it could have been via my feet—in such sultry weather we were inclined to wear open sandals or flip-flops. There may have been an abrasion or cut on a toe . . . only God knows. In the end, no matter how much of a turmoil my mind and emotions might be in, I had to learn to leave the incident with the Lord, along with the subject of my healing. Otherwise I could forfeit my inner peace.

With the PCP sufficiently under control I became an outpatient at the end of April, under care of the Royal South Hants Hospital. Arriving home at my parents' house, a celebratory photograph was taken to one side of the car. I had gained some weight, but my appearance was changed. While in Southampton my hair started falling out, sometimes in large handfuls. Consultants advised that the HIV virus can cause this, but it also frequently happens to those who have had a serious illness.

One evening I was trying to wash my hair over the sink, but the hair loss was really bad. Heartbroken, I wondered if I would end up completely bald. My youngest brother Keith heard me crying. He came into the bathroom and gave me a lovely hug. I realised how fortunate I was to be within a supportive and loving family, when so many AIDS victims are abandoned by relatives and friends.

Roy, my eldest brother, and his wife Jacquie, made an appointment with a wig specialist in Swindon. I could have obtained a wig through the National Health Service, but someone wanted to make a gift, so I bought privately. The hairdresser was patient and professional, and the fitting was confidential, in a cubicle in one corner of the salon. Brushed into a style, the chosen wig looked wonderful. I walked out into the street feeling great, if a little self-conscious.

'Where is it then?' asked Roy, who had been waiting in the car park. 'Did you decide not to buy a wig in the end? Your hair do's very nice.' He was not just being kind, he really hadn't noticed. Several months later my own hair had grown back enough to leave the wig off. It was such a relief to go without it. Though no one ever knew my secret I felt vulnerable, especially when shopping on rainy days in Salisbury market. There was always the fear it might be hijacked by a passing umbrella!

My health continued to improve after being prescribed the drug AZT, though I was kept on the lowest dose to avoid becoming anaemic. A pentamidine nebuliser helped the PCP, providing a fine spray for inhalation. Apart from dry, mottled skin and periods of tiredness, few signs of a fatal virus were apparent.

'Why you, Joy? Your life's been spent serving God and helping others. Why should you suffer in this way?' When they learned I had AIDS, questions like this started coming from many people. I had no pat answers then, or now, but rest in the confidence that God never makes mistakes. He called me and promised to be with me.

2

For as long as I can remember I have wanted to be a nurse. Coupled with this ambition has been a keen desire to travel, inspired by tales of far away lands brought to my parents' home in Wiltshire by visiting missionaries. Pentecostal Christians do not exactly believe in predestination, but a pre-school photograph taken in the 1950s shows a budding medic in best uniform holding my favourite toy Topsy, a black doll.

As I grew up the longing to be a nurse remained, though there was no confidence I would be able to gain the necessary qualifications. The thought of entering my father's business instead, the greengrocery trade, did not seem anywhere near as exciting. On reaching the fourth year at secondary school I sat an English Language RSA examination and, to my astonishment, passed. This encouraged me to stay on a further twelve months. Then came a two-year pre-nursing course at Salisbury Technical College. I managed to get the necessary credentials and began training to be a nurse at Poole General Hospital in 1968.

Three years later, soon after passing finals and qualifying as a State Registered Nurse, I attended an Elim Pentecostal Church conference in Blackpool. Among those speaking at a missions rally were a number of workers from Rhodesia. My memory fails to recall the names and faces of all the speakers, but I remember that a lively young teacher called

Mary Fisher was among them. She sang two hymns as solos and had a fine voice and I thought she looked youthful for a missionary—about the same age as I was. I had no idea then that we would one day be together in the same compound, or that she would lose her life in a terrible massacre.

Someone was appealing for doctors to volunteer for service in Katerere, as a married couple who began Elim's work there were reaching retirement age. I thought, 'I could never be a doctor, but maybe they can use a nurse,' and made my way to the front. A number of young people were gathering near the stage to dedicate their various careers to God. When it became obvious that no one was signing up nurses I joined this group, saying a simple prayer.

At the end of the week I went home and began pestering the Almighty about future prospects in a more fervent way. No definite answers seemed to come from above, but Dad offered some divine inspiration: 'It wouldn't do any harm to qualify in midwifery. Surely they'll need those skills in any developing country.' I joined a class in Bristol.

About a year later, when the course had just ended, I received an unexpected visit from the local pastor. A member of the Elim Missionary Council, he had recently returned from a meeting where the Mission hospital in Rhodesia was on the agenda. Matron Joyce Pickering was now the only expatriate there, and desperately overworked. In a letter she had written, 'If you can't find a doctor, please send a nurse with midwifery training.'

When I heard of this plea I had a tremendous feeling of peace. Though only twenty-four and fairly inexperienced, I knew God was leading me out to Rhodesia. The minister went to great lengths to explain all the problems I could encounter. Others tried to discourage me, saying I should wait a few years. In my simple childlike faith I was sure that if this was my calling, God would not let me down.

Once I had said that I was willing to go, everything

happened very quickly, with departure fixed for the last week of July 1974. The weekend before there was a farewell service at the Elim church in Salisbury, where it was touching to see nursing friends as well as regular worshippers. As I had been a Sunday school and youth group leader as well as a church member, three official presentations were made. With each came a Scripture reading, prayerfully selected by different people. No one had discussed which verse to choose, but all were the same: 'Have not I commanded thee? Be strong and of a good courage; be not afraid, neither be thou dismayed: for the Lord thy God is with thee whithersoever thou goest' (Joshua 1:9, KJV).

A ripple of amazement went through the congregation. God was making it clear to me, and everyone else, that he was sending me in his strength. It was a wonderful confirmation.

Although it meant travelling on a weekday, the whole family hired a minibus to see me off at Heathrow. Several friends were also there. In those days overseas assignments could last for many years. No one knew for sure when they might see me again. It was a bitter-sweet occasion.

'I still don't understand why you want to spend your life tucked away in some foreign country,' sighed Pearl, my younger sister.

'It's the role I want, just as that is yours,' I said, patting her pregnant tummy. 'I'll want to hear all the news of my new niece or nephew.'

'We're all so proud of you,' cried Mum, hugging my neck one final time.

Less tearful, Dad was concerned for my safety. 'We always thought you'd make a good missionary. Do exactly as you're told by superiors and don't take any risks. There are rumours of discontent and guerrilla warfare.' Behind his words were many shadows. I told him not to worry.

From Salisbury, Wiltshire to Salisbury, Rhodesia.

Although the flight lasted sixteen hours, elation kept tiredness at bay. Descending the steps on landing, a surprisingly cold wind blew around my legs. I began looking around for Alan Renshaw, the mission worker who was to meet me. As I pushed my trolley along after passing through customs and immigration, a deep voice called out: 'Miss Joy Bath?'

I turned and saw a tall, thin man with wide shoulders.

'You look just like your photograph,' he grinned. 'We'll have some lunch first, before setting off for Katerere—it's nearly four hours away.'

Alan is a good talker and time went by quickly as we covered the journey of 140 miles, mostly on bumpy gravel roads. I was conscious of passing through acres of quiet, flat land with no one in sight, just tall grasses on either side and mountain peaks in the distance. Now and again there were a few round, brown thatched buildings grouped together.

'They're called *kraals* and are the homes of village people,' explained Alan.

'The large houses in the city looked very grand and European. These are more traditional, what Africa is really all about. But I don't see any animals.'

'Not at this time of day, it's too hot for them. You'd have to come out here at the crack of dawn, or last thing at night. Of course, there are plenty in the game reserves.'

We came upon the Elim Mission in a valley at the foot of a small hill. Around 5.30pm, just before nightfall, I met Joyce Pickering and deposited my luggage at her house, where I would live for the time being. A cheerful but no-nonsense Yorkshire woman, she gave the instant impression of being an extremely capable and practical person; reassuring qualities to find in a matron. Over a grand meal prepared by Alan's wife Anne at their home, in honour of my arrival, the four of us chatted about ourselves and my new surroundings.

'Our complex here is like a little bush town, sprawling over 100 acres,' said Alan. 'Apart from the hospital there's the main church, also serving smaller chapels in the area, and the secondary school, of which Peter Griffiths is the Principal. Most of the teachers are away this weekend at a Scripture Union camp.'

Anne cut in, 'There are limited shopping facilities for basic food and clothing, African style, and you can buy cooking utensils and the like round here. But nothing resembles Marks and Spencer.'

'Joy seems to have brought sufficient suitcases!' laughed Alan.

'Perhaps it's time we unpacked some of the contents,' suggested Joyce.

After helping to clear away the dishes, Joyce and I hurried back to her house to put some of my clothes on hangers. Electricity in the Mission compound came from a generator, which switched off towards the end of the evening. There was about half an hour of power left. As I went to bed that first night in Africa the air was full of unfamiliar noises, including the sound of drum beats in the distance. It was disconcerting to realise I could no longer reach for the light switch.

'What was all that going on in the middle of the night?' I asked Joyce the next morning.

'Nothing to worry about—just a religious sect a way off who hold all-night meetings.'

'It's Sunday tomorrow,' I ventured. 'There's church for us, I expect, with or without the teachers?'

'There certainly is, and you're the special guest! By afternoon the teachers will be back. Today I'll give you a tour of your workplace and show you the house that will be your own after decorating.'

Most of the buildings in the compound were framed at ground level by neat gardens edged with white stones.

Exotic fruit trees—lemon, grapefruit, passion, pawpaw and banana—stretched their branches above tin or thatched rooftops. The hospital seemed very different and strange at first. There were far more staff than I had imagined. Trained nurses wore white uniforms and starched caps, while unqualified ones had blue dresses with white collars and cuffs. They all looked clean and smart, and greeted me with a polite, 'Hello, Sister Bath.' I shook that many hands and heard so many names I thought I'd never remember everyone. It was several weeks before I knew each face and name, and could match both together.

The following day, as I walked down to the Mission church, I imagined my parents attending their morning service. I was asked to say a few words and saw before me a sea of black faces, all friendly and smiling. It was enough to dispel any homesickness. I noticed that men and boys sat apart from the women and girls. The right-hand side of the congregation was sparse, as most of the men were away working, only coming home for holidays. The girls had fascinating hairstyles. Many had braids starting at the roots, twisted into different designs with black thread.

Other early impressions still remain with me. Nursing mothers carry their babies with ease on their backs in a special cloth called an *inbereko*. A crying baby receives breast milk immediately, whether Mum is on her own or in company. Families have new babies on average every two years. Older children help in looking after infants, and it is common to see three-year-olds with tiny babies on their backs, jigging them up and down to stop them crying.

That inaugural Sunday afternoon marked the first of many weekly visits for tea with Peter and Brenda Griffiths. They had worked with the founders, Cecil and Mary Brien, so I asked about the early days.

'The story begins in South Wales, in general practice in a

small Rhondda Valley town,' started Peter. Knowing this was a long yarn, Brenda reached for the teapot to refill our cups.

'The Briens were considering their future careers, and Cecil drove to Swansea one weekend, to take advice from Rhys Howells, founder of the Bible College of Wales. He was told: "Return home, and do what the senior partner at the practice tells you." Before surgery opened next morning, the boss rebuked him: "This preaching of yours in the streets of the town on your afternoons off is unbecoming to a medical man. You should go to Africa as a missionary." So he did as the doctor ordered!'

'Just like that, eh! But how did the Briens know where to start?'

'They didn't at first. They began by getting some experience at an established mission on the Mvura Dhona range of mountains, overlooking the Zambezi escarpment in the northern border region of Rhodesia. There they both worked as medics, learned the Shona language, and saw many people become Christians. After a time Mary Brien felt God was speaking to her through the Bible. A few verses just seemed to hit her in the eye, as if they were highlighted.' There was a pause as Peter reached for his Bible and thumbed through pages of the Old Testament to read: '"And the Lord spake unto me, saying, Ye have compassed this mountain long enough: turn you northward . . . unto a land that I will shew thee. . . . And they departed from the mount of the Lord three days' journey" (Deuteronomy 2:2–3; Genesis 12:1; Numbers 10:33, KJV).

'Cecil and Mary prayed together, asking for God's guidance. They also wrote to a friend back home, the Reverend Leslie Green. He replied almost immediately, saying they must leave their present posts and join forces with an Elim minister and his wife at a church in Umtali.

Around then, a white Rhodesian in the congregation there had a strange dream, which he told to that same minister, the Reverend Jesse Williams. It concerned a group of Africans from Chief Katerere's kingdom, carrying empty pots, looking for water.

'The Briens obeyed their message, even though it meant going south rather than north, and on a journey of two days, not three. Travelling in their truck, they slept the first night in Salisbury's Coronation Park, then drove on towards the Mozambique border and Umtali. Jesse Williams told them about the dream, and how it related to a region north of Umtali, in Inyanga North, where no missionaries had ever settled. Cecil and Mary were convinced that this was the place for them. However, they had to wait a while for agreement from the authorities before setting off to work.

'In August 1951 they eventually journeyed a third day and reached the Gairezi Valley in Katerere, where the road literally ended. Driving between trees and rocks, they came to rest on the banks of the Manjanja River. Now this stretch of water was reputed to be evil, the name meaning "stream of the lion spirit". Pitching their two tents they set up home, later adding a mud hut which became the dining room.

'Immediately they began preaching the gospel to inquisitive tribesmen in the Shona language, referring to Satan as the evil spirit, who took the place of God in people's hearts. "Jesus, his Son, will give you living water," they cried. The message had instant appeal. A young lad, Rhinos Mukwewa, became the first convert in the area. He is now a teacher and a leader in one of the local fellowships.'

'An inspiring story!' I commented. 'But what of their progress in medical terms?'

'It began slowly, as the local people were suspicious of

foreigners when it came to healing, preferring traditional methods. The Briens stretched a tarpaulin from the end of their truck over a framework of poles, and started a dispensary. Then there were clinics, where the Bible was opened, the gospel read and patients prayed over before treatment was given. They described to me their first operation, a herniotomy, performed on a table by the light of a hurricane lamp held aloft by an African assistant. Mary, the anaesthetist, put the patient under by dripping ether onto a mask. A valuable microscope was kept steady on top of Mary's ironing board. And things which needed to be cool were placed inside an old safe and submerged in the river until required.'

'The water comes down from the mountains, and the supply has never dried up, even in times of drought,' added Brenda. This was testimony in itself to the fruitfulness of the site. Still, I was thankful that working conditions had improved considerably since then.

'The Mission as it now stands is the result of Cecil and Mary Brien's faith and hard work. Nowadays there could be up to 1,000 people in the compound at times, wouldn't you say?' Peter rounded off the intriguing tale with a look towards his wife, which was also a signal to fetch more tea.

Established almost a quarter of a century before my arrival, the Elim Mission at Katerere had become well-known for miles around as a centre for health and education. In spite of this, I soon realised that the local witch-doctors remained a problem for the hospital. Highly respected members of the community, they had a real hold on people.

It was still common for sick people to go to the traditional healer first. Only if there was no improvement would an approach be made to us, and by that time the patient could be at death's door. Roots and leaves of various plants do have medicinal properties. The problem is that in

Africa's long, dry heat these become concentrated, poisoning instead of healing; the equivalent of taking an overdose. We tried explaining this to relatives of patients, but they still had more confidence in their own ways than ours. Many people died as a result, especially children. Their small bodies are more vulnerable to toxins.

There were no strict visiting hours in the hospital. Relatives of patients stayed at the bedside all day, and often slept underneath at night, if home was a long way off. If a person was seriously ill, and there seemed to be no immediate improvement taking place, relatives would assume the worst, asking that the patient be allowed to go home. There they could die in their own surroundings, with traditional rites being performed. We would argue against this—particularly as a longer course of treatment could often save the life—but it was not unusual for patient and family to flee the compound.

In spite of such disappearances, the wards and outpatients' clinic always seemed to be full of people. We dealt with virtually everything from infectious diseases to broken limbs and accident cases. And there was never a shortage of expectant or new mothers with tiny babies requiring attention. Efficient and businesslike, Joyce was panicked by nothing and no one. At work she was firm to the point of appearing stern at times, especially with the staff. In leisure hours she was just the opposite, and full of fun.

It was a relief to discover that all the Elim workers there were ordinary people. In my mind I had the misconception that they might be super-spiritual beings, giants of faith. I came to the conclusion that perhaps the great Christian pioneers—the first disciples, Francis of Assisi, William Tyndale, the Wesley brothers, Billy Graham, and maybe even Cecil and Mary Brien—were somehow different from myself and my new friends. The former were brave innovators; we just carried on with the work.

I was frequently tired, but always happy. With any new job come the staging posts of initial unfamiliarity, the feeling that one cannot absorb any more facts, and the gradual regaining of confidence as tasks are achieved and skills mastered. Through all of these I remained in a positive mood, feeling my role was the realisation of so many hopes and dreams.

3

The year 1976 saw a number of comings and goings at the Mission, beginning with the arrival of the Evans family in the spring. Philip was a teacher and the new deputy head, and Susanne had secretarial experience, which was needed for Peter's office. With them came their three young children, Timothy, Rachel and Rebecca (although the eldest two were later to be schooled elsewhere). The newcomers arrived twice: the first time they were refused entry on landing, and directed back to England. It seems Phil annoyed the authorities by declaring he would be a conscientious objector in the event of a civil war. Peter Griffiths managed to smooth things over.

Brenda Griffiths was suffering from insomnia. When the school closed for the Easter holidays, Peter decided to combine a check-up at the doctor's in Salisbury with his speaking engagement at a Scripture Union event near Bulawayo. He was confident that Phil could manage things in their absence, but wavered in this opinion after a worrying conversation with a member of the security forces. The latter operated a camp a couple of miles away and it was normal to see army vehicles driving through the compound. This time they stopped, seeking out Peter to bring news that two bands of guerrillas had come over the border from Mozambique. Perhaps he should think again about the trip. There might be trouble brewing.

'Political activists, some said to be Communists and

based outside Rhodesia, are stirring the native people up,' Peter told Phil. 'There's been no activity around here so far, but last year the school was visited by two terrorists—in civvies—as part of a general reconnaissance. They were members of the Zimbabwe African National Union.'

'But these boys may be from another faction. Whoever they represent, there's no guarantee they'll pay us a visit. And SU are expecting you—best not disappoint them,' Phil replied. So somewhat reluctantly Peter and Brenda put their things in the car and left.

The Renshaws and others were away on vacation. A single lady, Joan Caudell, was the only other expatriate teacher on site between terms. She was spoken to by a friendly contact in the security forces.

'The Avila Catholic Mission, not far from here, was entered by a group of terrorists,' she said gravely to Phil and Sue, relating the message. 'They were armed, and threatened people.'

'Was anyone hurt?' asked Phil.

'No.'

Peter and Phil had not told all of the remaining Europeans about their misgivings, only Joyce, and Roy Lynn, our caretaker. Now Sue was party to the information, she had disturbing tidings of her own to add.

'I heard some of the African women talking this week. There are freedom fighters in the district. I didn't think anything of the conversation at the time. Could they be a danger to us? I'm scared.'

Oblivious to all this, I was very much enjoying the company of my parents, who turned out to be intrepid travellers. This was their first visit to Africa, and together we climbed the hill behind the Mission for a clear view of the valley. It stretches as far as the eye can see, with the mountains of Mozambique in the distance. While up there we found some primitive bushman paintings, which fascinated my parents. Then Mum's mood changed.

'There's a man behind us,' she whispered as we began our descent. 'I think he's carrying a rifle.'

I turned slightly. 'It looks more like a walking stick. But even if it is a gun, he's probably out hunting.' The man kept his distance and did not bother us, but Mum remained uneasy. When we got back I had a shift to work in the labour ward and forgot the incident.

Meanwhile, Joan had moved in with the Evans family so she would not be alone at night. Ian Smith, the Rhodesian Prime Minister, was giving an important speech on the radio. They listened intently as he declared that the country was in a state of war, a fight for independence. His words added to their fears and all three of them prayed for God's protection before going to bed. The children were already asleep. Not long after the generator went off, the household was roused by a group of men shouting revolutionary slogans.

I was now living in my own place. I had given my parents my bed and was in a small guest room. Exhausted after a long and happy day, I had fallen into a deep sleep. Dogs are a useful addition to any missionary household, and Sandy, my alsatian–labrador cross, was a good security guard, disposer of unwanted reptiles and alarm clock. He could be quite fierce, and his loud barking woke me up.

'Who's there?' I shouted through the window. Sometimes the nurses would come and ask me to go to the hospital in the middle of the night. I could see no torchlight, and there was no reply to my call. Disgruntled, I scolded the animal and went back to bed.

Meanwhile, although he had only been in the country for two months, Phil Evans was doing remarkably well in talking his way out of a life-threatening situation. Refusing to open the door, he communicated with the callers by an open window.

'We've had enough of domination by the whites! We are the freedom fighters!' they declared. 'The whites passed laws which don't apply to them, saying we can't have guns, and must carry identity cards. We refuse to have cards, but we will carry guns!' Their weapons were raised in the air.

'This is a Christian Mission and we don't want to get involved in any fighting,' reasoned Phil. Then, in a flash of inspiration, he told them the story of how he was turned back at the airport for being a conscientious objector. This seemed to please the visitors. They calmed down a little, and listened until he had finished speaking. Phil could see white teeth in the darkness outside as they nodded their approval.

One man was not smiling. '"Love your enemies", "turn the other cheek", I know these are the words of Jesus, who also threw people out of a temple—as we will drive out the whites from our country,' he said, with real venom. 'Now, give me your medicines so we can treat our wounded.'

Sue handed over a First Aid box and the guerrillas backed off.

'Be quiet, you noisy dog!' I called to Sandy who was still barking, and I rose from my bed a second time. Hearing voices I went outside, wearing only my night-dress, expecting to see a couple of nurses. From the garden path a group of people were visible, congregating under the large branches of what I called the flamboyant tree. One of the nurses was there, plus an African teacher. The rest were strangers, wearing camouflage battle dress and carrying machine guns.

The nurse was asked to go to Joyce's house, which was close to mine, and bring her out to join us. She arrived breathless, but not from hurrying. It was the only time I ever saw her unnerved. The spokesman of the military group introduced himself as a freedom fighter, before launching into a lengthy speech.

'Eighty years ago the whites came. African warriors fought brave battles, but could not win without guns. We have guns now. We will liberate Zimbabwe!'

'Down with identity cards! Down with Ian Smith!' they shouted in unison. 'Down with . . .'

'Yes, we understand,' I butted in impatiently. 'So if you've finished we'll go back to sleep. I've been delivering babies, I'm very tired, I have to be up early tomorrow, and it's cold standing out here.'

'We know you help our people, so you will not be harmed,' replied the spokesman. 'But I have many soldiers—more than these here—and they need medicines and bandages.'

I looked at Joyce. Did he mean the compound was surrounded?

'Can't you bring your wounded down to the hospital?' she suggested.

'No, we must not be seen by the security forces. Come.' He pointed the way with his gun.

'Please let me go indoors to put on a warm coat,' I requested.

'Very well,' he replied. The group waited while I fetched my dressing-gown.

Walking to the hospital, we were told the freedom fighters had already visited Phil and Sue's house.

'What about Roy?' whispered Joyce, but she was overheard. There was a murmur among the troops, then the African teacher spoke. 'They haven't bothered him, because they know he has a gun.'

Roy's house was a little way from the others. He was probably unaware of our predicament.

We gave them everything they asked for, with me all the

time grumbling that it was most unethical to supply medicines without seeing the patients. Just before they disappeared into the shadows I was asked if we had a two-way radio.

'No,' I answered truthfully. Neither did we possess a telephone.

'If you tell the security forces about us, we will come back and kill you,' they warned. Then they were gone.

Joyce was shaking like a leaf. I suggested a cup of strong, sweet tea at my house with Mum and Dad. My parents! In the commotion I had forgotten they were there. Hearing the dog bark, they assumed I had been called to attend to a medical emergency. Dad needed rest and was asleep when we arrived back. At the start of their stay he had been disturbed at night when rain leaked through the thatched roof onto his side of the bed. Mum was wide eyed and worrying. A kind of sixth sense mothers seem to have told her something was wrong. As soon as I started relating it all to them, Mum remembered the man on the hill with a gun. Was there any connection? I didn't know.

When I was face to face with the freedom fighters I was not afraid at all. In fact I was indignant that they had come at night and woken me up. It wasn't until I started explaining what had happened to Mum and Dad that I began shaking all over. It was as if something clicked within me, and I realised Joyce and I had been in a very dangerous situation. If the terrorists had been drunk, or if they had taken offence at our words, they could have become angry. Who knows what they might have done to us?

I needed to read something from the Bible to calm my nerves and Dad's copy was handy. It was a Gideon publication, so he looked in the front index, where readings are listed for life's situations. Under the heading 'Where to find help when in danger' was Psalm 91. I took the book to read aloud, but became too emotional to continue. Dad carried on at verse 5: '"Thou shalt not be afraid for the terror by night; nor for the arrow that flieth by day."' The whole psalm was so appropriate. After a time of prayer together we all retired to our beds again. Mum, Dad and Joyce lay awake for the rest of the night. I slept like a log until morning, comforted by those words.

The next day we expatriates left Katerere for Salisbury, in several vehicles and at different times, so as not to arouse suspicions. Roy Lynn returned to keep an eye on things after escorting Joyce to safety. With hindsight I can see that it was unwise of us to up and go, but we were all inexperienced and nervous about the consequences of the nocturnal visit. Had we known our African co-workers better at that time, we would have realised they could be trusted. If we had confided in two leading pastors, Pious Munembe or Ephraim Satuku, they would have led us to make the right decision. The nationals could not understand why the missionaries had left so suddenly. This caused a slight distancing of relationships. I feel we failed them badly.

The guerrillas who had come to the Mission were cornered by the security forces a few days later. A number were killed, and the rest arrested and taken to Salisbury to stand trial. We all met for a conference to decide the future, and voted to return. The single ladies would be allowed to be in their own homes during the daytime, but would stay with the families at night. When Joyce or myself had to be on duty at night, one of the men would accompany us to the hospital and stay there until the work was done. This was tough on them as we could be up for hours, especially if there was a complicated birth happening. Also, the mosquitoes had a good feed as our protectors read by flickering lamplight to keep themselves awake.

The security situation began to deteriorate. Not many days would pass without us hearing of landmine explosions or encounters between terrorists and the authorities. However, all through the war no violence occurred within the Mission compound. It was as if all our prayers for peace in the midst of the hostilities were answered. Perhaps the surrounding circle of freedom fighters had been replaced by invisible angels.

One Sunday I returned from church and was cooking lunch when through the kitchen window I saw army vehicles arrive at the hospital. A civilian lorry had been blown up by a landmine and there were casualties needing immediate attention. The soldiers explained that there were no army medics in the area, so they had come to us for help. Peter took me to the scene with an African nurse. We travelled in convoy in his Peugeot 404. It was all right to be seen sandwiched between their trucks, but to sit with the security forces would lead people to believe we were taking sides.

By a little bridge near Kajozo an ancient five-ton truck was smashed and lying on its side. The driver was breathing his last. Nearby was a young man, moaning loudly. We parked some distance away in case the weight of the vehicles set off more mines, and walked back to the horrific scene. Behind us, the soldiers were watching the bush, guns at the ready, expecting attack at any time.

I ascertained that the man who was moaning had cracked ribs, and moved on. A young mother lay dead on the ground, with her tiny baby still at the breast. It was unhurt, though in need of nourishment. The slogan 'breast is best' is so true in developing countries. Feeding bottles are a death sentence if sterilising fluid cannot be bought, or incorrect proportions of milk and water are mixed. The water must be clean too. I wondered how this little ebony cherub was going to survive without a mother.

Another woman, still alive but unconscious, needed help first. Both legs were broken and bent the wrong way up from the shins, like a rag doll. Ants had already started to burrow into wounds around her heels. Scooping them out, we patched her up as best we could, putting on splints and setting up a drip. A man with a deep leg wound also required a drip. He had lost a great deal of blood. We gave injections of morphine to those who were in pain.

The casualties were taken away by helicopter, which made two trips and could not stay long in the area for fear of attracting the attention of guerrillas. I handed the infant to a rather juvenile co-pilot. He didn't seem to know how to hold a baby, so it was a new experience for both of them. As the chopper took off for the last time the pilot shouted, 'The doctor sends his compliments to the sister for a first-class job!'

The whole thing was a dreadful experience, especially for Peter, who was unused to seeing mangled bodies and had nightmares for months afterwards. We received feedback that everyone except the young man was doing fine. I was wrong about him and he died. He had a ruptured spleen, not cracked ribs. But at the time I examined him, his condition did not seem critical. Generally the person who is able to cry out is usually the least injured.

God works in mysterious ways. It might have been Phil Evans lying there. An hour earlier that Sunday morning he was driving the Mission's two-ton truck along the same road, with a group of churchgoers as passengers. Before reaching the bridge he mysteriously lost control of the wheel and slid off the road. No one was hurt.

On Tuesdays it was my habit to drive to a village called Kambudzi to hold a clinic. When Pastor Munembe told Peter that the place had become unsafe, he came to discuss the matter with me.

'I want you to make the final decision, but I advise you to

discontinue working there for the time being,' he frowned. As he stood before me I thought hard.

'Peter, those are poor and deprived people, in desperate need of medicines. I'll carry on running the clinic if you'll come with me.' He agreed, and became quite a useful form-filler in the process, while I carried on with the nursing.

During the first journey we anxiously scanned the road ahead for any signs of landmines, not realising we had already driven over one. We only became aware of it when an army truck behind us exploded. Thankfully the vehicle, unlike ours, was heavily reinforced. The only injury was to a trooper who was blown clear. He had landed on his rear end, damaging his coccyx.

At least one highway, to the district administrative centre at Inyanga, began to look like the lunar surface, with deep holes everywhere. Every so often this fifty-five-mile route was littered with debris, marking the sites where military vehicles had been blown apart. It was time to take certain precautions with our travel. The school lorry carried sand bags on the back and the tyres were filled with water. The Mission truck was fitted with metal plating. For the hospital, a hardy Rhino was purchased; a Land Rover ambulance offering more protection beneath our feet than most standard models. It was open at the top, until a tarpaulin was added, and looked like a white bath tub on wheels, with a red cross painted on each side.

We were instructed only to journey outside the compound by these specially adapted modes of transport, and not to venture out after dark. When going to particularly sensitive areas I had to wear a crash helmet and put cotton wool in my ears. Seat belts had to be worn on every trip. As the war intensified we had to contend with ambushes as well as the possibility of being blown up.

Peter was having a time of prayer and meditation one day when he felt compelled to read the biblical account of Ezra.

Part of the story concerns a journey to Jerusalem, past enemy lines. Ezra was too ashamed to ask the king for bodyguards, having previously declared, 'The hand of our God is upon all them for good that seek him' (Ezra 8:22, KJV). So he set off without a military escort, but arrived safely, reporting, 'The hand of our God was upon us, and he delivered us from the hand of the enemy, and of such as lay in wait by the way' (v 31).

Later on, I burst into Peter's office somewhat distraught, with a plea for help. 'I've a patient in labour who may need a Caesarean and can't be treated here. This is her tenth child, and the previous pregnancies have weakened her, so the uterus isn't contracting as it should. It may rupture. With a younger mother I could try fixing up a drip containing a drug to encourage the contractions. But I daren't risk it with this one.'

'Are you saying she has to be taken to Inyanga now?'

'That's right.' I was amazed by Peter's unusually calm manner. Night was falling. He knew the risks.

He said, 'Don't mind me sounding a little righteous, but God gave me prior warning of this. We have his permission to break the curfew.'

We went in the two-ton truck, with the patient and a relative lying down in the back. None of us dared speak for several miles and the silence was eerie. Coming onto the brow of a hill, my heart jumped. Fires were spreading across the valley below.

'It's nothing to worry about,' reassured Peter. 'They're just burning off the stubble in the fields—farmers do it every year about this time.'

Of course! I should have known that, coming from the West Country.

The journey was completed without incident and the woman taken to a government doctor.

Peter was required to report to the police station,

saying where we had come from, and giving the name of a hotel where we would spend the rest of the night.

'You were lucky to get through,' remarked the duty officer. The Principal of Elim Secondary School rose to his full, bantam height, determined to give credit where it was due.

'No, the hand of our God was upon us,' smiled Peter rather sanctimoniously.

4

'If any of us are killed in a landmine explosion, will we be classified as martyrs?' The question was hypothetical and said partly in jest, as a group of us met to talk about writing our wills and leaving instructions for funerals in the event of death in service. I felt I would rather be buried in Rhodesia to keep the costs down.

Suddenly, the blades of several helicopters whirred overhead. Choppers were landing in the compound. We rushed out to see what was happening.

'Civilian casualties, in shock, with minor injuries—nine young girls!' shouted a member of the security forces. 'We attacked a rebel camp, not realising they were entertaining their girlfriends.'

Joyce immediately sprang into action. 'Move the male patients into one ward to make room,' she ordered some junior nurses. Then she and I began giving the most badly shocked girls intravenous fluids. But we couldn't find any veins. Having worked in operating theatres in the past, Joyce had seen plenty of varicose vein surgery.

'I need to do something called an intravenous cut-down,' she explained. I marvelled as she made deep incisions around the ankles of two girls, in each case managing to find a vein.

Within a couple of days all the girls were feeling much better. They seemed popular, receiving visits from a number of smartly dressed young men. Later I heard that these were their boyfriends—rebels who had survived the attack. If the security forces had realised what was going on, we would have been in trouble for fraternising with their enemies.

Around this time road travel became so dangerous that Elim turned to the Mission Aviation Fellowship for help. Once a month a government doctor flew out from Umtali to an airstrip near Katerere. Leprosy sufferers received treatment close to the runway, before he made his way to the hospital to see any patients Joyce and I were worried about. Meanwhile the pilot was unoccupied.

On one occasion the doctor examined a physically small girl, who was due to give birth to her first baby. He confirmed our fears that a normal delivery would not be possible, adding, 'Sister Bath, Matron and I can manage without you for a time. Take this patient to Umtali in the plane. You'll be back before I've finished here.'

It was a windy day and the little Cessna was tossed about like a leaf. In addition, the pilot made swerving manoeuvres to avoid being sighted by terrorists. Some of them now possessed ground-to-air and heat-seeking missiles. The expectant mother had never been in a plane before and was terrified. I tried to reassure her, and held her hand most of the way, but was feeling green with travel sickness myself. We deposited her safely at the hospital in Umtali and had an uneventful return trip. To quell my nausea I tried to concentrate on the view, picking out landmarks. The white stones bordering Katerere's brown plots and pathways looked like rows of white teeth around open mouths, beckoning hungrily from below. A dentist's nightmare! Still, it was good to reach *terra firma* again.

The curtailment of journeys by land was unhelpful to Joyce's personal life. She and Roy Lynn were in the early stages of courtship and needed to spend time alone together off site, so they could become better acquainted.

Joyce did well to maintain a professional coolness at work, but I detected a warm glow around her whenever the likeable little Irishman was around. Roy was slightly disabled and walked with a limp. By way of compensation he'd been blessed with good looks and the gift of the blarney. Through knowing him Joyce had mellowed, and there was a spin-off into our relationship.

Joyce and I began to pray together regularly for the African nurses. It was her idea. 'Perhaps it will lead them into deeper spiritual matters,' she said hopefully. Although many were Christians they seemed oppressed by the war waging all around us. Some had reverted to carrying pagan charms for good luck. There had even been tentative enquiries about the end of the world coming soon. We decided to invite them to an evening meeting about the power of the Holy Spirit. Attendance was not compulsory, and the staff dining hall provided a non-threatening venue.

Almost everyone not on duty turned up to hear what we had to say. Joyce was about to start speaking when someone appeared in the doorway. There was an emergency in the labour ward.

'I'll go,' I volunteered, rising from my seat. The message of Pentecost would have more clout delivered by the Matron. Joyce opened her mouth to protest, but I was out of the room before she could say anything.

A couple of hours later a transformation greeted my return. Worried expressions had become wide smiles on glowing faces. Eyes shone and voices were lifted in praise to God. Even the room's atmosphere had changed. Many were sitting in small groups and from their lips came the gentle murmuring of different languages. People were speaking in tongues for the first time!

'The Holy Spirit has come,' sighed one of the ladies contentedly.

'Yes, and I haven't led this kind of meeting before,' beamed Joyce, with tears of happiness in her eyes.

I owned up, 'I'm glad you did, because I wouldn't have known how!'

Peace and joy flowed from that meeting, permeating every corner of the hospital for months to come. Only after Joyce and Roy became engaged, and she left on furlough to prepare for the wedding, did things sour. But the events were unconnected. I thought it was my imagination at first—paranoia brought on by extra responsibilities. Or could it be that some of the nurses were standing around gossiping about my marital status? Perhaps, like me, they were wondering whether a husband was going to appear on the scene. Eventually they came to see me *en masse*.

'We want more money,' said a spokeswoman.

I explained that they were all due for a rise in salary at the end of the following month.

'*I marii*—how much?' she asked. No one was impressed by my reply.

'That is too little,' said a second girl, while another threatened, 'We want more, or we will not stay here.'

'I'm seeing *mufundisi* Griffiths later. I'll mention the matter to him.' Sensing the group was becoming hostile I edged away, while agreeing to take the matter higher.

I was actually going to Peter and Brenda's for supper. When I arrived there they could see I was upset and were very supportive.

'The management committee, which takes advice from Africans, has overall responsibility for salaries. If the staff are not happy they must make a formal complaint,' said Peter.

'I think someone from outside's been causing trouble deliberately,' suggested Brenda. 'You know how Peter McCann is constantly losing things? Well, the other day the boy who works around the house went to fetch firewood, and hasn't been seen since!'

This raised a chuckle. Bearded and bespectacled, Peter McCann looked every inch the absent-minded professor. As a science teacher, he could not be faulted. In everyday living he was a complete scatterbrain, testing the patience of his wife Sandra to the absolute limit.

Brenda went on, 'It would seem the lad's been press-ganged into joining the freedom fighters. There've been a number of similar disappearances.'

'War is always hardest on civilians,' mumbled Peter Griffiths, momentarily becoming eight years old again and reliving German bombing raids on Swansea.

'There are staff problems at the school too,' said Brenda. 'The Renshaws are returning to Britain when their current contract ends. They have a number of family commitments to sort out.'

'But Catherine Picken is coming back here to teach English and sport,' replied Peter, returning to the present. 'She's been away looking after her elderly mother since before you arrived, Joy. And you'll not have to manage senior hospital duties alone for much longer. Wendy White will soon be here.'

After the meal I walked away from their house with mixed thoughts and feelings. The Renshaws were leaving. I would miss their cheery faces and helping hands. I pictured Anne Renshaw fitting Staff Nurse Evelyn's ample curves into a stylish wedding gown. An altered seam here, a pressed hem there, and a lovely head-dress of fabric flowers. The effect was topped off to perfection by a dainty parasol. Anne is like a fairy godmother to African brides. Over the years she has persuaded more than a score of Elim women in Europe to turn out from storage their precious white dresses, lying unused, and donate them to mission stations. Evelyn was marrying Pious Munembe and, as with most converts, wanted a white wedding 'like the English Christian girls'. Her chief bridesmaid looked lovely in a long dress loaned by myself.

That was my first experience of an African wedding and it was a day to remember. After a moving service, the reception was held outside the church. There was much singing and dancing in the hot sunshine. The guests sat at long tables and enjoyed a cooked meal of chicken served in a tasty gravy with the staple grain *sadza*—a versatile maize, on this occasion made into a kind of porridge. I was amazed that there was enough food to go round as it is not customary to send out official invitations for such events; the cooks just have to guess at how many to cater for. Every guest gave a present and the master of ceremonies shouted out what it was. This was followed in each case by applause and cheering, with traditional '*Rrululul*!' shrieking sounds, made by rolling the tongue. The whole process took several hours. Finally a family Bible was presented by Mai Satuku, in a flourish of low bowing movements.

Immediately after her wedding Evelyn became Mai Munembe. *Mai* is a respectful title for older women, who are generally always either married or widowed. The nearest word in English is 'Mrs'. Spinsters like myself, who are old enough to be married but aren't, pose a problem. There is no word in Shona to describe us. By default I have been addressed as *Mai* on many occasions.

I began to think about the new nurse coming out from England, Wendy White. Older than me, she would probably be called *Mai* as well, though she was single. I was looking forward to having an extra member of staff. But Wendy was newly qualified, a university graduate and social worker who had decided to switch careers in mid-life. There would be a lot for her to learn about coping with limited resources and facilities. Would she be capable, and willing, to take orders from me, a younger woman? I dearly hoped so.

A crowd of memories and expectations raced through my mind during the short walk to Phil and Sue's place. I was resident there at nights with Joan Caudell. It was surprising to see Sue outside the house with a bundle of something in her arms. I quickened my pace as it had started to rain. Sue was carrying a load of firewood, and I helped her inside with it. She explained how, like the McCanns', her hired help had also gone missing.

'I do hope those two haven't got themselves into any trouble,' she fretted. I watched as she shook her long brown hair loose from a pony tail. It was quite wet from the rain. Then she busied herself around the kitchen, sorting a pile of Becky's clothes for mending.

'You look really at home here, Sue,' I said, remembering how she had suffered from culture shock after arriving in Katerere.

'Oh, I am. Phil has always fitted in, but it took me a few months to carve out my own little niche. Now we're both sure this is the right place to be. We'll sit tight and ride out the storm, however rough it gets.' She referred simultaneously to the war and the downpour happening outside. The seasonal rains had come.

Three disturbing incidents shook morale at the Mission over the next few weeks. Everyone's faith and staying power were tested. In the south of Rhodesia an armed African in military uniform robbed a Catholic bishop and nun before shooting them dead. A second nun, who was able to hide, escaped detection and gave the authorities a description of the roadside attack and the attacker. In another part of the country a Catholic priest left his house to lead a service, but never arrived at the church. A search revealed no body or clues as to his whereabouts. Then, at a place called Musami, in the direction of Salisbury, seven Catholic mission workers were murdered.

It was with great trepidation that, a few days after this last event, Peter and Brenda Griffiths met Wendy White at Salisbury Airport. They felt duty bound to brief her on the latest developments in the war, giving her the option to back out at the last minute.

'The situation has become much more dangerous,' cautioned Peter. 'For the first time expatriates have been killed. We'll understand if you want to change your mind and return to England.'

The slim, elegant woman listened to what he had to say. Smiling graciously, head tilted to one side, she replied, 'It would take more than that to keep me from the Lord's work.'

Members of the Mission team were not prone to gossiping about one another, but everyone agreed that having Wendy around was like working with royalty. She was an exceptionally devout Christian, while at the same time being a lady from the upper classes: well-bred, well-spoken and schooled in social etiquette (an unusual and rather intimidating combination). She came with excellent references and was a good nurse, but had the annoying habit of always being right.

Shortly after Wendy's arrival I took her off compound to a baby clinic. Heavy rains had reduced the bush roads to rutted tracks of squelching mud, several inches deep. It was hard to drive the Rhino in such conditions. Even on dry roads strength and skill were needed for this vehicle, as the metal reinforcements had raised the height of the steering wheel. One almost had to stand upright to reach it. Consequently, I asked a male handyman—one of Roy Lynn's African assistants—to drive us to Chiwarira that day.

On the way back it began to rain heavily. When we reached a river bed that was normally dry, it had become a mighty rushing torrent. The driver stopped before attempting to go further. Should we wait for the flood to subside, or try to drive through it? Not wanting to be the one to make the decision, I left it to him. 'We'll go on,' he said, biting his bottom lip and looking rather worried.

Halfway through, the engine spluttered and stalled. We were stranded in the middle, and could feel the force of the brown flow buffeting the Rhino. The armour plating was watertight, but we began to move downstream.

'Help us, God!' I cried.

'We should praise the Lord,' declared Wendy.

I thought, *That sounds very good and spiritual, but what can we be happy about at a time like this?*

As if reading my mind, she said, 'Believe he is going to save us, and thank him in advance. Remember, "Faith is the substance of things hoped for, the evidence of things not seen"' (Hebrews 11:1, KJV).

We praised the Lord in English and in tongues for what seemed like a very long time. Mostly I didn't know what I was saying, but my heart was telling God that I didn't want to die yet. Nor did I appreciate his sense of humour in sticking me in a makeshift boat with Mary Poppins.

The water level appeared to be dropping. Trapped by mud, the Rhino halted. The driver rolled up his trouser legs, climbed out and waded to the bank. He reached it safely and waved to us before running off to fetch help. We were quite close to the Mission, so it wasn't long before he came back in a truck with Roy. They towed us out of the river and home to Katerere. Still the Rhino refused to start. Roy had to strip the engine right down in his workshop, to clear out the debris, before it could be used again. He was not amused.

I regularly wrote letters to my parents containing news of my experiences. They read the dramatic details of this account to my paternal grandparents and the facts were changed down the line. The next thing I heard was, 'Joy was sailing down the river and came face to face with an angry four-legged Rhino!'

In the meantime Peter Griffiths was in hot water with the security forces. Despite the numerous military skirmishes around the Mission, we believed we could continue our work through a policy of neutrality. The previous year we had had no choice but to hand over medicines when the freedom fighters visited. Since then, Peter had been contacted by guerrillas and had not informed the authorities. As a result he was arrested and found himself in court. His defence was as follows:

'News went along the grapevine that we were using vehicles which were reinforced against landmines. One of our ministers received a message, saying some guerrillas wanted to talk with me, and that I should preach at Kambudzi Church the following Sunday and await further instructions there. I was also told to take a collection among the teachers and bring the proceeds with me, to show good faith towards the rebels' cause. I took the service and afterwards shook hands with people at the door, as is our custom. Nothing unusual happened. I was just about to leave when Pious Munembe—the pastor, and headmaster of the local primary school—said there was a teenager waiting for me in the vestry. The young man had a note from "the comrades", telling me that he would guide me to them. When Pious heard this, he offered to go too.

'The three of us travelled in the cab of my truck for a couple of kilometres, until the lad said it was time to stop. We went on foot into the hills. Arriving at a clearing at the top of a slope we saw two sentries with automatic weapons. Then we came across a platoon of about a dozen armed combatants. I shook hands with them, greeted them in Shona, and went to sit down on the ground. Their leader told me to sit on a blanket, which I saw as an encouraging gesture.

'We were questioned for about an hour, mainly about why we had reinforced our vehicles. They saw this as a sign that we did not trust them to warn us if and when they planted landmines. I said that without a doctor it was sometimes necessary to rush patients off to Inyanga in the middle of the night, when there was no time to wait for warnings. They accepted this explanation.

'I suggested that if we stayed there much longer the security forces might spot my truck at the side of the road, and investigate. The platoon commander asked if I had brought the money from my teachers. I said that if I had asked for money, they would have become upset and might leave the school. Then it would have to close. However, I had brought $100, which came from the school funds. But this left me with a problem. How would I account for the missing money? As a Christian I could not lie, and neither could I enter into my financial statement, '"Gift to the comrades."

'Pious seemed to get a little nervous at this point, exclaiming, "Give them $50!" One of the combatants, who had been sitting on a tripod-mounted machine gun, came to the rescue by saying, "If he can't fiddle the books for $100, he can't do it for $50 either!" The commander seemed to understand, and we were allowed to leave without making a contribution.'

Pious backed up Peter's account, but the prosecution still wanted to know why the meeting had not been reported. Peter admitted he was guilty in this respect, but replied, 'Because I feared retribution on myself, Pious and the teachers. If that happened the school would be finished.' The court was lenient and Peter was freed. This time.

No one wanted to close the school or hospital. Both were providing vital services to the community. Yet we worried about what the authorities would do if the guerrillas made contact again. Then came a devastating blow which caused an urgent reappraisal of our whole position. The five-ton lorry, which was a lifeline for Mission supplies, hit a landmine on the way to Salisbury. Although heavily reinforced it was a complete write-off. The driver injured his back, and the man next to him—who was not wearing a seat belt—plunged through the windscreen and was killed. Another passenger lost a leg. Suddenly the reality of living in a war zone came too close for comfort. The vehicle was needed daily for bringing 1,000 meals to the school. The hospital sometimes used it for transporting large quantities of medicines and equipment. A replacement would be costly, and what if that were blown up too, with further loss of life?

Peter Griffiths was head of the Mission team, but the most senior Elim official in the country was Ronald Chapman, at Umtali. He attended a conference in Katerere with all of us, to discuss the future. Most were totally unprepared for what he had to say.

'Eagle Preparatory School is on the market for rental. It's in an area where there's been virtually no terrorist activity—the Vumba district—only a twenty-minute journey from Umtali. As Field Director for this part of Africa, I propose the secondary school moves there from next term.'

'That's a radical suggestion,' voiced Catherine Picken. 'What about the rest of the pupils?'

'The primary school mainly consists of day children and local teachers. It can remain where it is—there's no sense in uprooting people unnecessarily.'

'Brenda and I have been here about fourteen years, and are soon to go on furlough,' said Peter. 'I think this is the time for Phil to take over as Principal of the secondary school.' Phil looked at once pleased, unworthy and embarrassed. He began fiddling nervously with his spectacles.

'And the hospital?' I shrieked, the high tone of my voice reflecting the anxiety I now felt.

'It can become more of a clinic, run by less experienced nurses who live around Katerere. I understand Evelyn Munembe has sufficient qualifications to take overall responsibility?' Mr Chapman's eyes were staring into mine, demanding an answer. When I didn't give one, he continued, 'It may be the time, and God's will, for expatriates to step back and relinquish some of the work to capable, indigenous leadership. Not only at the hospital, but in the churches too.' He looked around at the collection of glum faces.

I found my voice. 'Yes, Evelyn would be an excellent choice. Wendy and I could . . . ?'

'No definite decisions can be made today. Approval will have to be given by Elim Headquarters at Cheltenham. However, the secondary school will need a nurse cum matron.'

'And a caretaker.' Roy Lynn entered the conversation. 'Joyce and I will be married by then. She could look after any sick pupils.'

Joan Caudell was also going on furlough. For her the choice was simple: she wouldn't be returning in the autumn. It was mooted that Wendy should fill the gap. She seemed very distressed at this idea, saying that while her degree qualified her to teach, God had called her to medical service. 'I'll have to think and pray about all this,' she scowled.

'And what about me?' I asked, almost in tears. Again Mr Chapman looked me full in the face. It felt as if everyone was staring at me, waiting for him to speak.

'You've been here almost exactly three years. Perhaps it's time to look for another position.'

5

Over the following weeks Wendy and I had a lot of heart-searching to do. The unexpected blow we had both received formed a common bond between us. Secretly we prayed that the proposed changes would be blocked by Elim Headquarters, and for a while it seemed as if the favour would be granted. Before his wedding to Joyce in Yorkshire, Roy Lynn represented Katerere Mission at an Elim Council Meeting. The members were unwilling to sanction the splitting off of the school from the hospital. However, it was agreed that their representative, John Smyth, would travel to Rhodesia to assess the situation.

By the time he arrived Wendy had made her peace with God. 'If the decision is made to move to the Vumba, I will take it as the Lord's will for me to go there. After all, I am qualified to teach English and History,' she told me.

'At least you've had some choice as regards your future,' I replied bitterly. Wendy shot me a reproving glance. Still feeling hurt and angry, I could reach no such plateau of acceptance that my first overseas assignment was coming to an end.

When John Smyth saw how things were, he began to realise it was in Elim's best interests for the school to be sited elsewhere. Individually we were all given a chance to say what we felt, before coming together to hear the verdict. The earlier recommendations were confirmed. I had no option but to obey orders and start packing for home. I was heartbroken.

Before the August holidays a second-hand lorry was obtained to ferry load after load of furniture and non-essential goods to Eagle School. On about the sixth trip it hit a landmine. Thankfully, no one was hurt. The engine was destroyed and the cab windows were blown out, but the rest of the vehicle and its contents remained intact. A breakdown truck arrived, complete with military escort, to tow the lorry to Umtali. Unfortunately the driver was none too careful on the dirt roads. Probably driving too quickly in order to get out of the danger zone, he rolled our lorry and did what the landmine had failed to do, completely destroying it and the load.

At the end of term, three buses came to take the boarders to Umtali. From there they would travel back to their homes. About fifty miles down the road the first bus hit a landmine. Two students, Leonard and Daniel, were killed. A third boy, Jotham, lost a leg. Terrified, the remaining youngsters clambered onto the other buses. The second one arrived safely, but the third bus hit another mine and caught fire. Everyone was able to escape through the windows, which had blown out in the explosion. The driver was the only fatality. For the final clearance of essential equipment and personnel the services of a furniture removal firm were hired, protected by a heavy military escort.

A few days later Mary Fisher and I started a memorable holiday in Durban, South Africa. We seldom saw the sea as Rhodesia was land-locked, and we really appreciated a fortnight spent largely on the beach. While we were relaxing in the sun, our peace was shattered by the tragic news of a huge bomb exploding in Woolworths in Salisbury. Eleven people were killed. How long could this carnage go on, we wondered?

Mary was apprehensive and nervous about teaching in the new location. Her large eyes opened even wider in anticipation, as she described the whereabouts of Eagle School.

'It's very close to the Mozambique border. A beautiful setting, high up in the mountains, where the climate is cool and damp—*Vumba* means misty. The tourist guide books liken the area to England's Lake District.'

'Better take your wellies, then,' I advised. Having Mary around was good therapy. Her incessant chatter helped me to come to terms with the fact that I was leaving. And she was such an innocent it was impossible to hate her for having a job I couldn't do for lack of the right qualifications.

To have another string to my bow would prevent me from being in this kind of difficult situation again, I considered. After completing my midwifery course I had toyed with the idea of going to Elim Bible College. Now the opportunity presented itself again. I took this as the way forward and, back at the Mission, enrolled by post for two years of theological study.

Then it was time to say *chisarai zvakanaka*—goodbye—to Rhodesia. I arrived home on 25th August 1977, to be met by a crowd of family and friends. Three years had passed since I'd seen most of them, and everyone was talking at once, trying to tell me something different. A niece had been born to me via Pearl, and here she was, Charlotte, already walking and attempting to join in the conversation. Travelling back to Wiltshire in the church minibus, I did my best to catch the excitement of the moment, but I had a throbbing pain in my head, and ached all over.

Mum had prepared a huge spread for the whole family. I just wanted to have something to quench my thirst, and then go to sleep. The following day I felt worse and had a high temperature. The doctor was called, and he prescribed antibiotics. It was thought I might have flu. Somehow I managed to get to the hairdresser's, and then went on to a big homecoming celebration at church. Attendance was mandatory as the Mayor and Mayoress of Salisbury were guests of honour. Afterwards I collapsed into bed and stayed there. Four days later jaundice started to make itself evident. The doctor came again and hepatitis A was diagnosed. It took a number of weeks to recover, which made me late starting at Elim Bible College.

The two years spent in residence there in rural Surrey were of tremendous benefit in many ways. My relationship with God took on a new dimension. At that time the college was housed in an old mansion at Capel, set within large grounds. There were plenty of places and opportunities for private reading and contemplation. Good thing too, as I had to share a room with three and sometimes four other students.

Settling down to full-time studies was not easy. I found it difficult to concentrate, and the long hours spent poring over books resulted in eye strain. In addition, there were practical jobs for students to do. At first I was on the cleaning rota, which meant one work period before breakfast and a longer session each afternoon, vacuuming long corridors. I hadn't regained my strength from the hepatitis and by the end of each day was completely exhausted. Later I was given lighter duties serving in the dining room, for which I was grateful.

Fellow students didn't quite know how to treat a real live missionary. Some tried to put me on a pedestal, or treat me like a china doll. Determined to show I was normal, I went out of my way to be involved in as many pranks as possible. Water fights and dunking people in baths of cold water soon showed them my true colours.

I was surprised to find little zeal for overseas mission among the theological students. A conversation with one young man left me particularly disturbed. His main objection was that in the middle of the jungle there would be nowhere for him to go for dental treatment if he developed toothache. This seemed a worrying lack of faith and common sense in someone training to be a pastor!

There were a number of foreign students at Elim Bible College then, including a white South African, and black Africans from Kenya and Guinea Bissau. During the holidays it was possible to take one or two to my home. It was fun for them to meet the family and learn Wiltshire English. When winter came they were fascinated by snow—something they had not seen before. One even went outside to roll in it.

As the temperature dropped and strong winds blew around Capel, I reluctantly put away my cotton dresses and brought out thick wollens which hadn't seen the light of day for four years. Still it seemed unbearably cold. Then someone had the bright idea of placing polythene sheets over the windows—a primitive form of double glazing which effectively cut out some of the draughts.

Peter and Brenda Griffiths returned to England shortly after me. It was to be a period of study leave, so that Peter could complete a post-graduate degree. The three of us met at Heathrow to see the Lynns off. Joyce's parents were also at the airport to say farewell. They were concerned for the well-being of their daughter and new son-in-law, even though Eagle School was thought to be in a quiet area, safe from Rhodesia's warring factions. Roy's expertise was badly needed for maintenance work. Joyce would conduct clinics locally when her medical knowledge was not required by staff and pupils.

A selfish little voice inside me was saying that I should be on the plane too. I tried to ignore it. The pair looked so happy and right together. Something Joyce said gave me a hint that she might be pregnant. It was odd that they went through the departure barrier without looking back for a final wave or glance. Peter noticed this too and remarked on it.

I didn't see him or Brenda again until Saturday 24th June 1978. A Midsummer Day etched in my memory for all time. But I was aware that Peter had been sent back to Rhodesia in the spring for a few days, as there were fears of unrest in the Vumba district. On his return, he told me by letter that everyone was happy and wanted to stay at the new site, where they were at least safe from the threat of landmines.

He wrote: 'We came to the firm conclusion that as the school and the young lives in it were important for the future of the country, the work must continue.' Roy—who had experience of living in the strife-torn areas of Northern Ireland—was adamant that 'mission workers just can't keep running away'.

However, the murder of two Salvation Army teachers working in the country, plus a series of anonymous threatening notes sent to our personnel, persuaded Headquarters at Cheltenham to instigate further changes. Elim International Missions Director Leslie Wigglesworth instructed Ronald Chapman to ensure that non-African staff left the school after lessons each day. Accommodation was to be found within the urban safety of Umtali.

The last Saturday in June was Elim Bible College Open Day and Graduation Day for final year students. Peter was to give the address, and planned to speak on the true story of a group of missionaries in Ecuador who were murdered by Auca Indians. Late morning I was busy with last-minute cleaning jobs. A voice came over the tannoy, 'Will Joy Bath please report to the Principal's office.'

I had no idea why I was being summoned, but hurried along there. When I entered, the room seemed full of members of staff and foreign students. The atmosphere was tense and people were looking around nervously. One or two were crying. Wesley Gilpin, the Principal, welcomed me with a nod of his head. Then he began to speak.

'I have to tell you all that a dreadful massacre took place last night in Rhodesia, in a remote region near the Mozambique border. I don't have all the details yet, but it is suspected that the victims were our mission workers.'

My initial reaction was one of peace. It couldn't possibly be my former colleagues, because they had gone to live in Umtali, only commuting to Eagle School during the day. But over the next few hours, as information filtered in from Ronald Chapman and various news networks, it became clear that it was our people. Their belongings had been packed into cases, and the workers were scheduled to move into new homes the following morning. Instead, as dawn broke, their dead bodies were being discovered on a grassy bank near the sports field. The attack was so violent that some were almost unrecognisable.

By the cricket scoreboard lay a mature woman with dishevelled clothing, including a yellow cardigan. In one hand was clutched a matching scarf, which she had intended to put over her greying hair to conceal the fact that she was wearing curlers. A long-handled axe was embedded in the back of her head. Catherine Agnes Picken: an overseas veteran with eighteen years of fine service to her credit. She first worked in the Belgian Congo in the 1950s, but left there because of ethnic troubles.

A young man wearing a trendy purple sweater and trousers was found with his hands tied behind his back. His face had been split open. Philip George Edward Evans: BSc, Phd. Two weeks earlier a premonition had prompted him to send an album of precious family photos to his mother for safekeeping.

The face of another man had been bludgeoned by a piece

of wood. But his beard was still visible. Peter McCann: BSc and former student of Elim Bible College.

Spread-eagled on the ground was a woman in a blue top and slippers, her left arm stretched out towards a tiny baby. Eileen Joyce Lynn: SRN, midwife and newly delivered of her own child, Pamela Grace. How often I had watched and learned from our resourceful Matron, a cheeky lock of dark curls poking around the side of her cap as she worked. Her hair was now matted with blood, and beside her the daughter born just three weeks ago had been bayoneted to death.

A few yards away a man in a checked shirt was found, horribly mutilated. Robert (Roy) John Lynn: an Elim Bible College graduate. His eyes had apparently been gouged out, and his body was riddled with knife marks. The man who had refused to run away from trouble had been stabbed in the back at least fifteen times.

Then there was a group of two women and three small children: Susanne Eugena Mary Evans with Rebecca, who was four-and-a-half years of age; and Sandra McCann with her son Philip, aged five, and daughter Sharon Joy, four years old. All had been beaten about the head viciously. One of the youngsters had the imprint of a boot on her face. The mothers also had bayonet wounds around the neck, and were naked from the waist down.

Under a tree in a nearby copse a young woman in a denim dress, with long dark hair, was huddled in a foetal position. Elisabeth Wendy Hamilton White: SRN, BA, Dip Soc Stud; daughter of a supermarket magnate and granddaughter of the man who pioneered the Mersey Tunnel. Her murder was possibly the most gruesome. She was severely beaten, and bayoneted in the head, neck, chest and groin. That would probably be because she angered her captors by telling them about Jesus. Eloquent Wendy would not have gone down without a verbal fight.

There was one piece of good news. Mary Fisher: triple graduate of Swansea, Brunel and London Bible College, was still alive! A trail of blood led the security forces to a patch of long grass, where she had run to hide. Unconscious and hypothermic, she was rushed to hospital in the capital and placed in intensive care.

Twelve martyrs, and one brave soul fighting for her life. What kind of mindless beings could have sent my guileless friends into eternity so brutally? Whose politics could demand the savage crushing of young skulls, the raping of women and little girls? And why did no one come to their rescue? For some time I was too shocked to cry—my emotions were kept at bay by a questioning mind. I needed to know more.

It transpired that a large group of guerrillas had attacked the school after supper on the Friday night. Some gave the pupils a talking to in the dormitories, while others herded the British teachers out of their houses at gunpoint, to a quiet spot. The noise of the killings, away from the buildings, failed to reach the ears of a South African teacher, Ian McGarrick, who was in his room marking examination papers. It was he who made the grim discovery of the corpses early on that Saturday morning.

By early afternoon my mother arrived at Capel. Though deeply distressed, she kept saying, 'Thank God you weren't there! You're safe!' This finally brought out my grief. The two of us collapsed into a heap and cried for several hours.

The formalities of the day went ahead, but even now I wonder how Peter managed to stand up and speak. The main theme of his talk remained the same: believing in Christ is no insurance policy against death through missionary activities. Only the names of those who died were changed. Instead of mentioning Americans, his words were of our own dear folk.

Many memorial services were held over ensuing

weeks. And one verse from the Bible was repeated again and again: 'Except a corn of wheat fall into the ground and die, it abideth alone: but if it die it bringeth forth much fruit' (John 12:24, KJV).

Suddenly, the Elim Pentecostal Movement was at the centre of world events. British and foreign governments, Ian Smith, and leaders of other churches, were all discussing the massacre, adding to the already substantial amount of media coverage. The publicity resulted in many hundreds of volunteers coming forward for overseas service. If interest in missions was lax during my first year at Elim Bible College, the situation was totally reversed after the events of 23rd June 1978.

Tragically, Mary Fisher never regained consciousness and died in hospital. This brought the total number of martyrs to thirteen. People began to remark on how my life had been spared. Was it for some special purpose? I didn't think too much about it then. I never thought my lot would be to go through a different kind of martyrdom. My thoughts and heart were directed towards the families and relatives of those who died. In particular Timothy and Rachel Evans, who woke up one morning at boarding school to find they were orphans. I was only made redundant from my job. They had suffered a much greater loss.

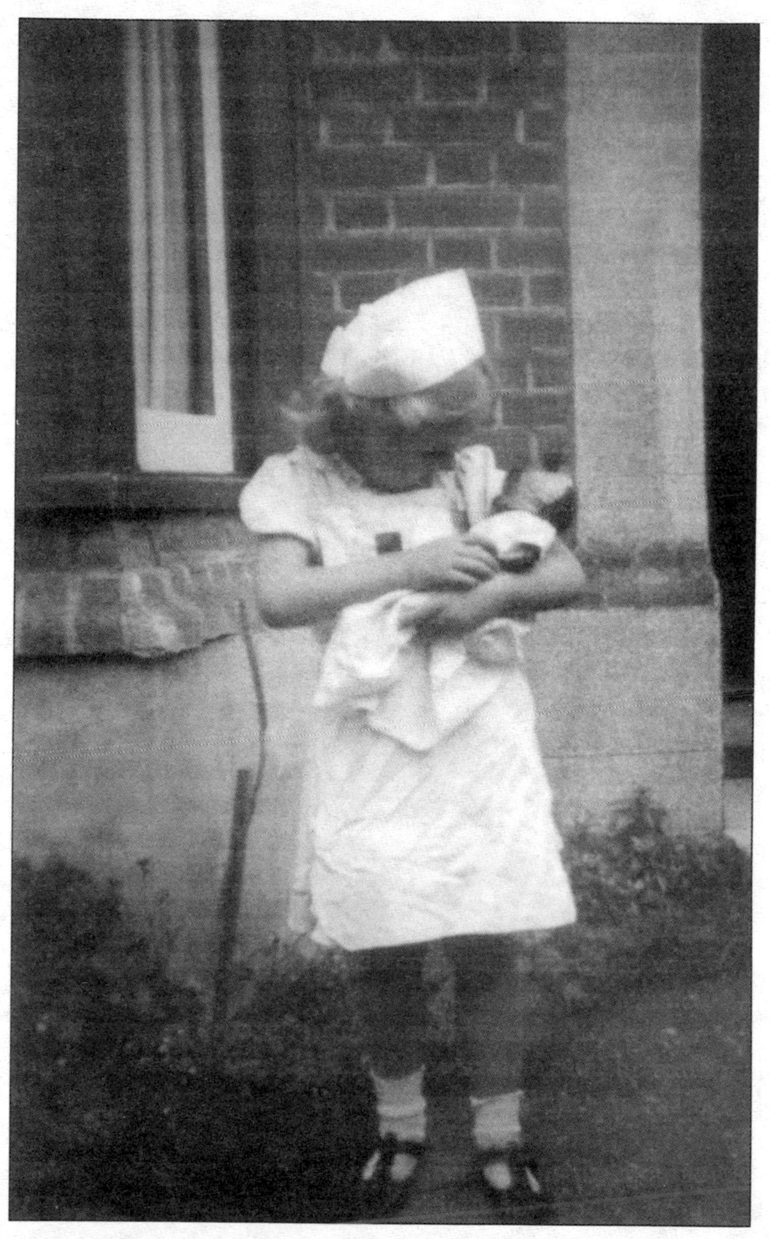

A budding medic holding her favourite toy, the black doll Topsy.

Carrying a baby the traditional Zimbabwean way. Sandy the dog looks on.

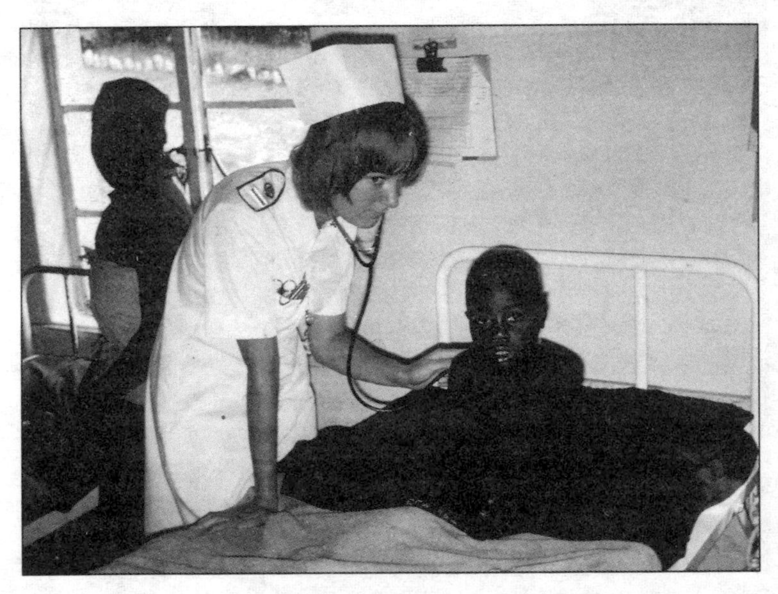

Her first term of service: learning to manage with limited resources.

The main Elim Church in the compound at Katerere.

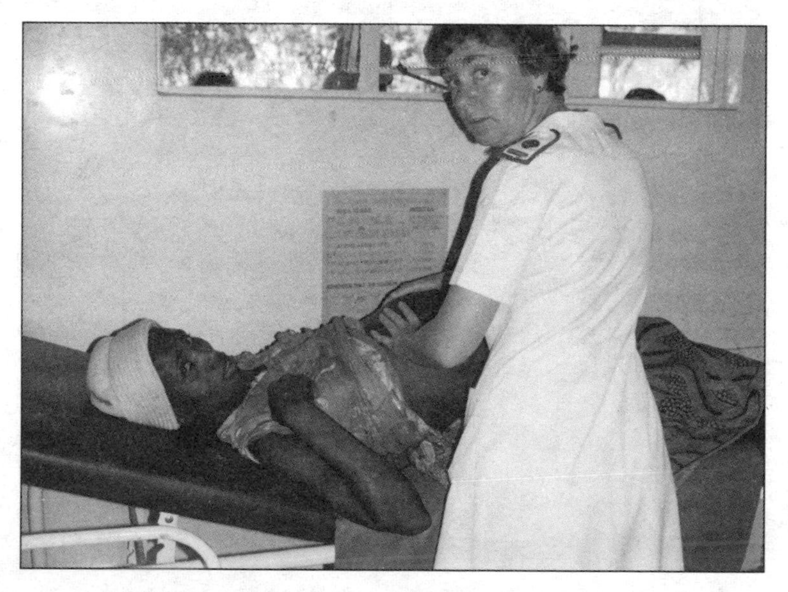

Examining a maternity patient during her last term of service.

At home in the Bath family garden, Wiltshire, 1994.

6

What next? Towards the end of year two at Elim Bible College I was interviewed about my future plans. The Missions Board would not consider a return to Rhodesia. The situation was still dangerous. But there was an opening at a small clinic in India, with scope for gospel ministry. It was mine if I wanted it, but I wasn't sure. My feathers were still ruffled from the pain of being told to leave Katerere. And the loss of my friends weighed heavily on my heart. I thought and prayed about the offer for some weeks, before finally deciding to accept it.

On 11th July 1979 I found myself at Delhi Airport, being met by the small, motherly figure of Olive Jarvis. There were people everywhere, making a lot of noise as they went about their business. I could hardly hear what she was saying for the constant hubbub of excited voices—absolute bedlam. An overnight stop in a hotel provided some peace and quiet. Then it was back into the crowds again and on to the railway station for a 600-mile train journey to the state of Bihar.

Our compartment was full to overflowing, with bodies pressed together on all sides. Some alighted at each stop, but they were replaced by more people getting on the train. It was extremely humid. Such air as there was contained pungent smells. Though I had done my research and knew the population of India totalled over 700 million, the reality of being confronted with a large, jostling portion of humanity was claustrophobic.

It was impossible to avoid making comparisons. Africa is a continent of contrasts—luscious foliage or sun-bleached grasses; modern cities versus wide open spaces. Tribesfolk are distinguished by different physical characteristics and forms of dress. To my untrained eyes everything in India just seemed brown. From the houses to the burnt sienna dust of the roads and railway tracks. The people were mostly the same colour brown and as the majority were poor, so were their once bright clothes: browned with age and accumulated dirt.

Olive watched my reactions with a bemused expression on her face.

'This is the main train route to Calcutta, so it's particularly busy. Bihar is one of the most densely populated places in the world, and one of the poorest areas of India. I've been out here for twenty years and have grown used to the way of life.' There was a pause as the train halted. Vendors with grubby fingers pushed baskets and trays of refreshments through the open windows.

'Be careful what you eat and drink,' she advised. 'You could easily pick up a tummy bug. Even the bottles of water with screw tops probably aren't safe—they tend to fill them in the river.'

I wasn't tempted. Both food and liquid were brown too.

We were based at Dehri on Sone. A tiny, typically Indian town, without street lights or pavements. A high wall surrounded the only church and we went through large iron gates round the side to our single-storey house. It was divided into two: one part belonged to the Indian pastor, the remainder was shared by myself, Olive and a third worker, Sylvia Beardwell.

The house had few amenities. Electricity was fitful and often went off, or was too weak to be of any use. We frequently resorted to candles or paraffin lamps. Running water was only available at certain times of the day, otherwise it meant a trip to a hand pump in the yard. Even when the water came on it was always cold—there was no hot.

We did have a nice walled garden, full of flowers. From it went a raised pathway through paddy fields to the dispensary, our place of work. This was also surrounded by a high wall. The place was primitive. Just one room divided into two was used for consulting and giving out medicines. Opposite was a shelter where women and children waited to be seen.

For cultural reasons it was not possible to see men. And we could only treat minor ailments as there was no doctor or equipment for anything else. Coughs, sores, impetigo, scabies, ringworm, diarrhoea and ear discharges were common. The patients were very poor, in various states of distress and illiterate. We had to find a way of keeping them in line or the last would push to the front and an uproar would result. A system was devised so the first ten who arrived were given blue cards, the next red and so on, to ensure they waited in order.

Usually the clinic was finished by midday. In the afternoons it was necessary to rest, due to the heat. But in the evenings we sometimes went out on visits, or else I would keep busy with language study. What a triumph it was to master the alphabet! Without it I couldn't even board a bus unless I asked someone for its destination—and most people didn't speak English. The first hymn I learned in Hindi was 'How great thou art'. It was very popular at that time, and sung at most meetings.

Sylvia was younger than Olive, but both ladies were quite a bit older than I was. In Rhodesia the expatriates formed a closely knit community and I enjoyed friendships with a variety of age groups. Here there were just the three of us foreigners, apart from a Scots lady who also resided in the town. Living so closely together, personality clashes and differences of opinion due to the generation gap would erupt now and then. I realised it was important to put things right as early as possible, before they were blown out of all proportion.

Olive was very kind and patient in helping me to adjust to my new environment. Diminutive but businesslike, Sylvia undertook to educate me in cultural matters. I believe this exercised her mind as well as my own.

'The reason we see so many ear patients is close breeding,' she told me one day. 'There is a social structure of castes. The main ones are *Brahmin*—the priests and their families, *Kshatriya*—warriors, and *Vaisya*—merchants. The three are not supposed to mix. Officially, discrimination is banned in this country, but it's part of Hinduism to stay within one's caste, and as most Indians follow that religion, marriages happen within family groups.'

'Aren't some people outside the castes, for example the Christians?'

'Yes. The tribal people tend to be Christian or Muslim. The *Harijan*—the untouchables—are technically the lowest caste, but many have become Buddhists. Sikhs have their own ways and customs, and would like to have their own independent state. They form a very small part of the whole population and are mainly found in the Punjab, to the north west, on the other side of Delhi.'

I found all the Indians intelligent and hard working; even those begging on the streets. But there was a gap in their mentality when it came to crossing social barriers. Not long after that lesson from Sylvia, I saw the dead body of a man lying in the middle of a Dehri on Sone street. It remained there for several days and was decaying by the time a member of the same caste came to take it away.

Some people might liken this situation to the story of the Good Samaritan. It reminded me of one of the opening scenes of a film, *The Magnificent Seven*. An outcast had died, and someone provided a coffin, but the undertaker and his men were too scared to take the body away for burial. They feared they would be shot by racially prejudiced townsfolk. Enter the Christlike hero Chris (played by Yul Brynner) and another brave soul called Vin (Steve McQueen). They drove the hearse, dodging bullets and shooting back at their attackers, until they reached the cemetery gates. A stirring moment in the history of moving pictures.

On another occasion I saw a man severely beaten by way of religious persecution. It stands out in my memory, happening in a land where all beliefs were supposed to be tolerated. However, at Christmas a subtle form of intolerance was shown towards Christians. Buying cards with a nice message was not easy, as most didn't mention the actual festival. Probably the makers were trying to avoid using the Lord's name. 'Season's Greetings' was the norm.

Carol-singing was popular with young church members. A group would set off after dark, cycling around the town and stopping at Christian homes. After singing they would be given food like sweet meats or *samosas*—triangular pastries filled with good things—before moving on. There was much merriment, and the visits went on late into the night. Christmas Day was a public holiday, but as most shopkeepers and market stall holders were Hindus or Muslims, it meant business as usual for them.

The climate was very unkind in Bihar. Summers were too hot and dry; the monsoon season was too hot and wet. With the rain came clouds of mosquitoes. My legs were always covered with bites. Winter was a welcome respite. The only complaint was that it didn't last long enough—only for about four months and then it was back to the burning heat again.

It was a relief to spend our holidays at a hill station.

There we had the company of other mission workers, and I spent a few hours each day at a nearby language school. The station was really a spartan cottage, with limited bathing and toilet facilities. We stayed there for about six weeks each summer to avoid the worst of the heat. In the hills the temperature stayed a little cooler, but not much.

To reach the station took a whole day. It involved a train journey, followed by a hair-raising ascent up a zigzag road in a taxi with bald tyres. I closed my eyes so as not to see the sheer drop either side of the steep track. Vehicles could only travel so far, and the last part of the climb had to be made on foot, carrying luggage and all. Once we arrived, it was necessary to fumigate the premises; rats having been the only occupants since our last visit.

Becoming more proficient in Hindi meant I could take on a Sunday school class at Dehri Christian Church. It was fun and when words failed me, actions and visual aids were used to get the message across. Compared to English children they were extremely well behaved.

I also began venturing out to see needy families on my own. A Muslim man was employed to look after the garden and drive our rickshaw—a three-wheeled bicycle with a seat at the back for passengers, and a hood to keep off the sun or rain. Once, on the way to a village, he turned off the main highway onto a side road, pedalling fast.

'Help!' I cried, as I fell out and landed on my head in a ditch. Hearing footsteps, I expected the rickshaw *wallah* to come and pull me out. But he just paced up and down the road until I hauled myself up. It was a long wait, as I suffered slight concussion and felt very dizzy.

'Why didn't you give me a hand?' I demanded angrily.

'It is not the custom for a man to touch a woman,' was the reply. Then he admitted sheepishly, 'But I have done another kind of wrong. I knew there was a problem with one of the wheels before leaving Dehri.'

When we arrived at our destination some villagers kindly made me a cup of tea as I was still giddy. And I was supposed to be ministering to them!

The visit of a delegation from Elim Headquarters caused a lot of excitement. John Smyth and David Butcher flew in from Delhi to a domestic airport. Olive and I went to meet them in a jeep with a hired driver. At some point on the way there the horn failed, so on the way back we stopped at a garage to get it fixed. While no one seemed to check on tyre conditions, it was illegal to drive without a horn. In India you need the horn all the time. We were certainly glad to have it working later on in the journey.

Ambling in the middle of the road was a herd of elephants. Not wild ones, but transport animals for wealthy people. The passengers were sitting on top. A keen amateur photographer, David Butcher gleefully reached for his camera to catch the unusual sight on film.

'We pose for you,' volunteered the elephant handler in Hindi. He seemed an obliging sort and the passengers were good natured, so John Smyth and I also took some snaps.

'You're very kind. Thank you. Enjoy the rest of the trip,' I said as we prepared to leave. At this, the handler began to get agitated. Arms waving in the air, he ordered the elephants to kneel down, completely blocking the road.

'I don't think they'll move unless you pay him!' laughed Olive.

She was right. We tried blaring the horn for some time. The noise attracted quite a crowd, but the elephants stayed put. We had to give in and pay up before we were allowed through.

The presence of the two visiting pastors meant evangelistic meetings could be held in Dehri on Sone. The Indian minister didn't do much in that line, and as the culture held no great respect for women, Olive, Sylvia and I were restricted in what we were allowed to do.

'We three are absolutely powerless!' moaned Sylvia during a private meeting with John Smyth and David Butcher.

'We're certainly not using the full range of medical and theological training we possess,' I chipped in.

'All we can do is pray,' said Olive.

The pastors agreed and we took time to bring the matter before the Lord in prayer.

Unbeknown to us, God was calling a man from South India—Augustine Jebakumar—to begin a major work in the North. The first we knew of it was when he arrived at Dehri on Sone with a small group of workers, including two young women. They said they were called the Gospel Echoing Missionary Society, GEMS for short, and began working within Dehri Christian Church.

Talented and enthusiastic, they were like a breath of fresh air through the district. Unfortunately, the staid members of Dehri Christian Church felt rather intimidated by their presence. In addition, jealousy developed over funding obtained from overseas for evangelistic campaigns.

God does not only use Christians in the furtherance of his work. A *Brahmin* lady was so impressed by the GEMS that she gave them five acres of land as a gift. It was in a country area, with plenty of room for expansion. The team moved out of town and set up on their own. One of their young women left to be married and I made a real and lasting friendship with the remaining girl, Jeya. We became like sisters. It was great to have someone of my own age to relate to.

After being unwell for some time, Sylvia was sadly diagnosed as having cancer of the bladder. She was flown home to England as treatment in India was difficult to obtain. I was working more and more with the GEMS team and feeling that was where the main thrust of my work should be. It made sense for Olive and me to close the dispensary and join the GEMS at their base. They had started an orphanage, and were about to open a school.

A number of business people had approached the GEMS requesting that a mission school be set up. Standards in government and private schools were poor and it was generally accepted that mission schools provided a high standard of education. Augustine asked if Olive and I would be willing to teach. As nurses we had no experience or qualifications to be school teachers, but no one seemed to mind. I became a teacher of English and Environmental Science, learning how to teach from books. The children were lovely and well disciplined. I felt fulfilled and really enjoyed the experience.

Two pieces of advice I still remember from those days are: real teaching is guidance—helping a pupil to find the answer themselves; and if a lesson hasn't gripped the teacher, it won't interest the child!

Once again, political events had a hand in changing the course of my life. In 1984 India's Prime Minister, Mrs Indira Gandhi, was assassinated by Sikh extremist members of her bodyguard. All foreigners without visas were ordered to leave. That included me. It was a hurried departure, but I believed that obtaining a visa was just a formality.

'I'll soon be back,' I told Jeya confidently.

'I'm not so sure, my friend,' she replied. 'Getting official papers sorted out can be a slow process at the best of times. Now the country is in mourning . . .'

Indians can be highly emotional people at times. I decided this was one of those times for Jeya, and chose to ignore her forebodings.

Once home I made an application to the High Commissioner of India in London, requesting a long-term visa. It was refused. I appealed against the decision, backing up my case with letters of recommendation from influential people in India. I never received a reply.

As time went on it became apparent that I was not going to be able to get back. I took a Teaching English as a Foreign Language course in London, and then a short course on tropical diseases in Liverpool. After this, as I'd been out of full-time nursing for ages, I joined a nursing agency in Salisbury, Wiltshire and for a year eased myself back into my favourite profession.

'I don't know where I'm heading, but I don't think I'll ever be returning to Africa,' I told a friend. The reply was, 'It's best to pencil in your plans for the future. Then you can always rub them out if God has other ideas.'

7

With the spring of 1987 came an unexpected summons to Elim Headquarters at Cheltenham. Brian Edwards had become Director of International Missions and was eager to meet with me. I had assumed he had in mind a general chat about my situation, but it wasn't long before the conversation with this tanned, rather suave man began to centre on Katerere.

'A lot has happened in nine years, Joy. Life in independent Zimbabwe, as the country's now called, is very different.' I nodded in agreement. He went on, 'Under a new government the health service has developed, and that is good. In practice it means more primary healthcare, ante-natal clinics and infant vaccinations. There's also an emphasis on family planning, and attempts are being made to curb the spread of AIDS.'

Leaning forward in an animated manner, he started tapping one end of a ball point pen on the desk. 'Staff at the Elim Hospital are run off their feet serving a population of about 60,000. Apart from the national workers there are currently three Brits there—a doctor and two nurses. A third nursing post has just been made available via the authorities. Can I put your name forward?'

Of course I said, 'Yes!' It was more than I could ever have hoped for.

After all the formalities were completed I flew out to South Africa in July, to be met by Peter and Brenda

Griffiths and their two sons. From there we travelled to Zimbabwe, with hardly a silent moment passing between us. I had a lot of catching up to do.

'Salisbury is now Harare, Umtali is Mutare, and Inyanga is Nyanga,' chanted the boys in unison.

'Katerere's stayed the same, in name anyway,' laughed Brenda.

The family had returned to Africa, so that Peter could resume his important work of helping to educate young minds.

'The last time we met was at a youth camp on the Isle of Wight,' I reminded him. 'Not long after the massacre.'

'Yes, let's fill in a few gaps. After coming out here to help prepare for the funerals, I spent some time arranging for the transfer of students to other schools. Although secondary school places were at a premium at the time, people were sympathetic. Places were found for all 300 children, albeit scattered throughout the length and breadth of the land. Splitting them up was providential. Many were able to start Christian groups in schools where none had existed before. But that's not all. Do you know of a lady called Janet Cunningham?'

'Vaguely. Didn't she start an organisation for women?'

'Yes, Homemakers. Well, she invited me to speak at a combined meeting of several groups of Homemakers on the subject of forgiveness. This had become a controversial issue since the media quoted various Christian relatives of our dead colleagues, speaking of forgiveness for those who murdered their sons and daughters. You see at the same time, the average white Rhodesian was crying out for revenge.'

Brenda took up the story. 'Peter was due to fly back to England the day before the meeting. He said he couldn't attend. Then Janet spoke to him again, and the next thing I knew, he'd delayed his departure by two days. She must be a persuasive woman!'

'Ah, but it was the right decision,' emphasised Peter. 'In my talk I pointed out that whatever we think about the idea of forgiveness for murderers, Jesus prayed that those who crucified him would be forgiven. Although we may not be murderers, we are all sinners, and all need the forgiveness of God found only through the cross, when we repent and call out to Jesus to save and forgive us. I made no sort of emotional appeal for people to commit their lives to Christ, but did point out that anyone interested in becoming a Christian could leave their name and address in a book after the meeting.'

'Did anyone?' I asked.

'Yes. Six ladies.'

There was some significance in the number six. Up in the Vumba mountains, God had allowed six grown women to be martyred and find entrance into his heavenly kingdom. Now I was hearing that after the very first external meeting since the massacre where Peter was able to speak of God's offer of forgiveness in Christ, six women had come forward. A shiver went down my spine.

As we came nearer to the Mission memories came flooding back and I went quiet, trying to control my emotions. A few obvious changes had been made, like new houses for staff, but no extra buildings had been added to the hospital. There were still some members of staff I remembered from before and I was amazed how the lilting Shona language all came back. Nurses who didn't know me had quite a surprise when they realised I could understand their conversations.

Dr Adrian Smyly was a primary healthcare specialist. He put a lot of effort into building up the preventive healthcare services to the community. More baby clinics were established and called ZEPIs (Zimbabwe Expanded Programme of Immunisation). They took place in fifteen different locations, including Nyamombe Refugee Camp, a two-hour drive from Katerere. Ante-natal and post-natal care were introduced at the ZEPIs, using the back of a Land Rover ambulance as an examination room.

It was marvellous to see the improvements in healthcare. In the 1970s we had treated sick children every day of the week, but other services were only available once a month. Now parents could bring their children from Monday to Friday for weighing, vaccinations, and treatment if they were sick.

A real bond of friendship and teamwork developed quickly between myself and the other two expatriate nurses Debbie Brown and Bobbie Marcus, the Matron. Evelyn Munembe had given up full-time work in order to have a family, but she was still active in the community whenever possible.

The days were busy and happy, like those during my first term of service before the civil war. If my thoughts strayed too much towards the massacre, there was always some job or other to be done around the hospital to occupy the mind. I wouldn't admit it, but I was putting a lid on deep emotional hurts.

Before returning to Zimbabwe I told a friend who is a journalist, 'God has forgiven the murderers, so I must too. I feel no bitterness towards them.' I meant what I said, but when the words came out in print and I read them, a great gaping sadness welled up inside me. Every now and again, during quiet moments, those words would come back, echoing around my head.

In June 1988 Mary Brien visited the Mission. Her husband had passed away, so she came as far as Nyanga with a nephew, before being collected by Bobbie Marcus and a group of ladies from the church. They travelled in an open pick-up and we heard their approach from some distance—

the ladies were singing a song of welcome with great gusto. People came running to the vehicle to greet her.

She was with us for five days, and from the time of her arrival until the time of her departure there was a constant flow of Zimbabweans waiting to see her, singing to her and bringing gifts. On the Sunday morning the church was packed with people wanting to hear her speak. She was an octogenarian, but had plenty of energy to stand and preach the gospel, and she gave an appeal at the end. It was a real thrill—for her and the expatriates—to see so many men respond. Some had made commitments years ago, but had grown indifferent. Others made a stand for Christ for the first time that morning. After the service a party took place outside the church. Representatives of various chapels and groups in the area sang songs and gave their appreciations to her.

I know it is wrong to put people into little boxes, but I marked Mary Brien down as being an old school type; a woman with a strong personality and full of determination. She was staying at Bobbie's house and had problems with the door keys. On finding herself locked in, she was seen climbing through a bedroom window one morning at 6am. Nothing was going to prevent her from joining the nurses for early morning prayers!

Any antagonism I felt towards Mary Brien was undoubtedly due to the fact that she had sussed me out. Somehow, she knew I needed healing from memories surrounding the massacre. We didn't talk much, but she urged me to pray in the manner of her late husband, 'Lord, help us to live in the light of eternity.'

Then it was the tenth anniversary of the massacre. Bobbie and Debbie were suggesting a trip to the Vumba. It was rare for all three of us to have days off together. Oh, how I tried to avoid going, and how glad I was afterwards that I went with them. Sometimes one has to be dragged out of the past in order to face the future.

Each of us had a profoundly moving experience as we stood by the graves of the martyrs. The plots are marked by simple white crosses and surrounded by specially planted jacaranda trees. An eerie stillness pervades the clearing, though it is a beautiful resting place.

Suddenly the silence was broken by the sound of violent sobbing. I realised it was me. At first it was as if someone else was crying and I was an onlooker. I sank to the ground. Cradled in the arms of my friends, there came a point of owning emotions I had suppressed for so long. A part of me had died and was buried with the victims. I needed to grieve.

When I was all cried out, the three of us stood and praised the Lord for bringing us together to work in Zimbabwe. In turn we rededicated ourselves, declaring our commitment to God, whatever it might mean. Then we sang two hymns: 'Here I am wholly available' and, remembering Mary Fisher's voice on flexidisc, 'For me to live is Christ, to die is gain'.

We turned to leave and Debbie remarked, 'They weren't so much heroes as those who simply believed they were called to do a work, and to carry on doing it until told otherwise.'

Bobbie was frowning, 'In my book that's exactly what heroes are.'

The scene from that old Western flashed through my mind's eye once again. 'They were our magnificent thirteen,' I mumbled.

Feeling fresh and clean, I fell silent on the way back to Katerere. I was thinking of some of the great paradoxes of the Christian life. Of Stephen, the first Christian martyr, who, although young, had an amazing ability as an evangelist, only to suffer death by stoning when he was being most effective for God. And James, who, as one of the inner circle of Jesus' disciples, received special revelation and training, only to be killed most brutally by Herod. Even more puzzling was the fact that after Herod arrested Peter, he was rescued by miraculous intervention, only to die for his faith later in Rome. I wondered why his life was spared on the first occasion.

I had been hearing rumours for some time that the man who led the rebel attack on Eagle School was now a Christian. There was formerly no desire within me to investigate the matter further, but the healing experience by the graves had stimulated my curiosity. At a convenient moment when visiting Peter Griffiths at home in Harare, I asked if he knew anything.

'Oh, plenty,' he said, with a mysterious smile on his face. 'I've been waiting for you to say something, but you weren't ready before.'

'Is it true?'

Peter nodded. 'The man, Gary Hove is his name, attended a Bible college here in the city. He wants to be a preacher.'

'You've met him?'

'We've had several chats. I'm sure his conversion was real.'

Peter went on to tell how, one Sunday morning just after Independence, Gary Hove was reading a newspaper in his room at an army camp in Bulawayo. His eye caught sight of an article in bold type, which commenced with the words 'Dear Comrades . . .' in bold letters. It was actually a paid advertisement inserted by a missionary called Margaret Lloyd, telling of the love of God towards everyone. Then it described the conversion to Christ of a Cuban Marxist called Raphael. At the end was a PO Box number.

'Gary read the piece aloud to some of his buddies. They

were all angry that a comrade, albeit a Cuban, should become a Christian. It was decided that Gary should write to Margaret, inviting her to meet all of them so she could answer questions about the Christian faith. This was a ploy on their part to lure her to the camp and kill her. The letter was written, and Gary put it into the thigh pocket of his fatigues.' Peter demonstrated the movement with his own hand.

'Walking to the mail box in the camp, his hand went to his pocket. The letter had disappeared! He couldn't remember exactly what he had said before, but he hurriedly wrote a second letter. By reply, Margaret sent some Christian literature and a Bible. He not only read what she sent him, but also began to visit churches.'

'Hungry for God,' I asserted.

'One night, back at the barracks, Gary and his friends shared a strange religious experience—a vision—in which they all saw a cross. Then Gary alone saw the hand of God coming down, as if in judgement, to smite him. He cried out to God for mercy, and asked to be saved from his sins!'

'Incredible!' I exclaimed. This was some story. 'It's just like Saul of Tarsus, who tried fervently to crush the early church, only to find Christ himself, and to become Saint Paul.'

'After the first time I met Gary, I arrived home to find an unexpected visitor—one of my ex-students—Colin Kuhuni.' Peter looked at me as if I should know this name. I didn't, and said as much.

'Colin is a bright young lawyer, trained to sift through evidence and look for facts. He happened to have been a student at the school when our friends were killed. Along with the other pupils, Colin was subjected to a propaganda talk from Gary and his platoon. I told Colin about my meeting with Gary and the story of his conversion. Immediately I had finished, Colin asked, "Tell me what he looks like." This wasn't difficult, as Gary is so tall and angular. When I gave the description Colin said, "He was the man who lectured us on that dreadful night." It seemed that God had brought Colin along that day to confirm I had met with the right man.'

'Phew! Did you question Gary about the massacre?'

'The second time we met. Apparently the whole thing was a revenge attack—there was nothing personal in it. Gary and twenty others carried out the murders in retaliation, after the security forces killed some of his people. I plucked up the courage to enquire how the missionaries reacted when they knew they were going to die, and what they might have said. His reply was that they prayed God would have mercy on their murderers and save them.'

Once again a shiver went down my spine. Almost as an afterthought, Peter said, 'One of the women—it had to be Wendy—shouted something like, "You can kill our bodies, but not our souls." '

Brenda came in at that point. I had taken up an entire afternoon of Peter's time, when he should have been looking at students' papers. After kissing them both fondly, I started off on the long drive back to the Mission.

The moon was up and full by the time I reached Rainbow Cottage, the little house which had been built for me. It was so called because the decorators had painted each room a different pastel colour, which was extended to the outside window frames. There was time for a toasted cheese sandwich before lights out. I chose to eat it by the blue window, enjoying the moon, and the stars which had come into view beside it. I pictured how those graves in that eerie Vumba clearing would look on a night like this.

'Yes, it would have been Wendy,' I said to myself, then went to bed.

8

Adrian Smyly's term of service came to an end. Everyone was grateful for the improvements he had brought to the Mission hospital's Maternal and Child Health Department. Over a period of eight years the numbers of children treated increased dramatically from 5,000 to over 18,000. In his place came Roger Drew, a young surgeon. He took one look at the operating theatre and declared, 'Some of this equipment is all right. I suppose the rest belonged to Cecil Brien. He probably bought it from Noah!'

The theatre was brought up to scratch, and we were able to do even more for the people of Katerere. Our inaugural major operation was a Caesarean section, performed in the middle of the night. It was the first of many, and we became quite expert. I gave the anaesthetic, Debbie would help with resuscitation of the baby, and a medical student assisted Roger. We had some failures. There are many risks to mother and baby during pregnancy and the birthing process.

One heavily pregnant patient came to the clinic with a vaginal discharge. I gave her something for it, but the infection refused to clear up. It was diagnosed as having been sexually transmitted. Although she had been delivered of several children already with no complications, this time the poor woman was growing larger every day, with no signs of going into labour. We let her go over ten months, hoping for a normal birth. But the baby grew too big for a vaginal delivery, and a Caesarean section was performed. This was risky because of the infection, but there was no other choice. The baby died, but the mother survived. She was tested and found to be HIV-positive.

We were continually aware in our work of the steady increase of AIDS. In 1990, 132 new patients were HIV tested at our hospital. Fifty-three of these were positive and five died during the year. In 1991, 199 were tested. Eighty were positive and fourteen died. Most of the infections were passed on through heterosexual relationships. Some patients were infants who had contracted the virus from their mothers.

I mentioned earlier that many of the men travelled to large towns and cities in order to find work. They came back for holidays and special occasions. In between times prostitutes satisfied their sexual desires. Many of the women already had AIDS from unprotected sex—often with customers such as truck drivers, who travelled to and from distant parts of Africa. When the men arrived home the virus passed to their wives, and any subsequent offspring. There is a cultural practice in Africa for widows to marry a member of their dead husband's family. As infected women were paired with previously uninfected partners, AIDS gained more victims. In some parts of the continent whole communities have been wiped out.

Eventually every patient at the Mission hospital was treated as potentially HIV-positive, whatever the diagnosis. To protect the staff, rubber gloves were available. We didn't have enough to use new ones with each patient. The gloves were washed, soaked in bleach and dried. Staff were also encouraged to wear rubber gloves when putting up drips and taking blood samples for the laboratory. Nurses were careful to wear heavy duty gloves when handling soiled laundry, and plastic aprons and gloves when changing bed linen.

Faced with the prospect of an early death, some people will try anything in the hope of finding a cure. A married couple from Harare came to Katerere, having heard of a tribesman using herbs on AIDS victims. The husband was very ill and this form of natural medicine made him worse. As a last resort, the wife brought him to us. Bedridden and seriously dehydrated due to continuous diarrhoea, there was little that could be done. The man died. If he had been admitted earlier, oral rehydration might have prolonged his life.

His widow was left with the awful problem of having to transport the corpse back to Harare. Tradition dictated that he must be buried in a family plot. She had no money, so I arranged for the body to be taken to a mortuary at Nyanga. There it could be kept in a refrigerator until she had the funds for the next stage of the journey. I thought that was the end of the distressing story, but after the wife had left with the body—weeping and wailing as is the Shona custom—in walked a daughter. She was unaware of her father's death. When I told her the sorry tale she became hysterical, violent, and had to be restrained.

In some places AIDS patients are treated as outcasts. In Katerere relatives are generally supportive. It is essential that families receive spiritual and medical help when patients leave hospital. An AIDS home visiting team was set up by the Mission hospital to enable the dying to be nursed in their own homes. The team is led by Mr Chitima, a church lay worker, assisted by Mai Sagwidza. She had previous experience in the Mission hospital's Rehabilitation Department. Qualified nurses administer medicines and whatever else is required.

This can involve the washing of open sores with soap and

water, or salty water, which acts like a disinfectant; giving fevered patients bed baths of cold water to help cool them; and rubbing aching muscles with soothing coconut oil. Paracetamol is often used as a painkiller. Other remedies utilise resources available locally. For example, the juice of a sliced onion mixed with sugar makes an effective expectorant for a dry cough. Packets of oral rehydration salts are used in the hospital for acute cases of diarrhoea, but for mild cases four teaspoons of sugar and half a teaspoon of salt, added to a litre of boiled water, will do just as well.

Family members learn simple but important skills, like how to turn a weak patient over to avoid bed sores. They can alleviate the discomfort of thrush in the mouth by providing salt water mouthwashes several times a day. The giving of moist meals containing tomato, banana and other kinds of juicy fruits and vegetables, provides vitamins, replaces body fluids, and at the same time helps to soothe sore mouths and throats.

I saw a number of youngsters orphaned through AIDS. The lives of others were touched by the deaths of brothers and sisters, aunts or uncles. One way I could reach out to these children was through Sunday school classes. Mai Simango, a Zimbabwean lady of about fifty years of age, was my partner in this venture. She was a boarding school mistress at Penhalonga, before obtaining a similar post at Elim Secondary School, which had now returned to Katerere.

For their own good, Mai Simango ruled the older children with a rod of iron. But she was very kind and loving to the little ones. They would flock around her buxom figure, seeking a cuddle, like chickens under the wings of a mother hen. When I went to her house to plan lessons we would always end up on our knees. Mai Simango was a woman of great prayer.

On a larger scale AIDS education became part of the

general school curriculum. To take effect, the best approach was to give advice at an age before the children became interested in the opposite sex. Older pupils, whose natural passions were already aroused, were less likely to listen to reasoned arguments. Adults, particularly leaders of communities, were targeted through talks and seminars.

For some time Bobbie Marcus' state of health had been a cause for concern. Little had been said in public, though members of Elim churches in Britain and Northern Ireland were aware she had been undergoing tests. She didn't have AIDS. The symptoms related to her mobility and nervous system. Multiple sclerosis was one possible explanation. She was flown home, where more tests revealed a less serious problem. Happily, she fell in love with Pastor David Tinnion and they were married. Bobbie never returned to work in Katerere.

Her departure led to an important event in my life. Saturday 18th February 1989 was highlighted in my diary as a day off. Nothing significant in that. However, the morning was disrupted by a visit from Brian Edwards and Peter Griffiths. The two had arrived at the compound the previous evening and we shared a meal together. It was a pleasant enough occasion, with no sinister overtones. Now they wanted to talk business. Why? In the kitchen I poured coffee for the three of us, and took it through to the lounge. Brian appeared tense as he took a cup.

'Joy, the hospital needs a new Matron,' he began. 'Evelyn Munembe is back, but with a family of her own to look after, she can't take on a full-time job. Debbie isn't quite ready yet, we feel, to take on overall responsibility. And none of the Zimbabwean nurses has enough qualifications for such a role. But someone else does.' As Brian paused to take a sip of black coffee I caught Peter's eye. He winked at me.

Brian continued, 'We—that's myself, the Missions Board

and Peter—would like you to have the post of Sister in Charge here at the Elim Mission Hospital.'

So that was it. An ordinary day had suddenly become rather special. My heart was beating faster as I replied, 'I'd like that very much. I hope I'll be worthy of your trust.'

I shook hands with Brian and received a fatherly hug from Peter. Then it was over to the hospital where Pastor Ephraim Satuku and Roger Drew confirmed the appointment. The rest of the day was spent writing letters home to tell members of my family the good news.

Official announcements were made at the hospital the next day, and prayers were said for me in church. I said my own private 'thank you' to the Lord—the one who put a yearning for nursing and Africa in my heart from childhood. I was on cloud nine and stayed there for several months, until the rains came.

It was mid-November. While driving to Harare one day to collect various supplies, my vision blurred as my head began to swim—with the heat, or so I thought. Concentration was difficult and I had to keep repeating to myself, 'Salaries from the bank, pick up lactogen, enquire about parcels.' A dark cloud followed me back to Katerere, but no rain fell.

A couple of days later I was having supper with Roger and his wife when a dramatic storm came on. We viewed it from the verandah. The lightning was quite beautiful to watch as it forked down the sky. The noise of the rain was almost deafening as it landed on adjoining tin rooftops.

'Good,' I sighed. 'This will clear the air, and hopefully my sickness.'

'I thought you'd been looking a bit pale,' said Roger. 'Is everything all right?'

'It's nothing really. Just a muzzy head and general malaise. Despite taking medication, the symptoms have persisted.'

The change of weather brought no relief. The following day I vomited and immediately felt better. About a month later, while on duty in the operating theatre, I started to feel ill again. If it wasn't the heat this time, perhaps the condition of the woman lying on the table was to blame. Attacked with an axe, she had suffered terrible head wounds. Was I experiencing a surge of emotions in a flashback to the injuries described at the Vumba massacre? No. Hours later, feeling hot and feverish, I popped a thermometer in my mouth to discover my temperature was up. I mentioned the matter to Roger, and was taken aback by his reply.

'You're off on holiday soon. Have a complete and thorough medical, including blood tests.'

'But I'm sure there's . . .'

'No need to worry? Maybe not. But whatever it is, it won't go away without proper treatment. Look, I don't want to scare you, but with all these AIDS patients coming in—you should have *that* test too.'

I was going home for my brother Tim's wedding. Shortly after I sailed through a check-up, and an HIV test showed me to be negative. I heaved a sigh of relief and returned to Zimbabwe. The sickness did not recur. From time to time most members of staff went through a period of anxiety about contracting AIDS. Roger had a particularly nasty scare.

A small boy was admitted, complaining of abdominal pain. A bowel obstruction seemed the obvious cause and Roger began an operation. No bowel contents were found, but the lymph nodes were swollen and bleeding. This could indicate typhoid, tuberculosis, lymphoma—or AIDS. Two nodes were removed for further investigation, and the boy was closed up.

Roger told me, 'The wound was sutured, the dressing neatly in place. I turned my attention to the instrument trolley. All the needles were stuck to an adhesive pad in their container. They had been new, we'd just received them from England. I went to close the lid of the container to make it safe for the nurses who would soon be clearing up. One needle wasn't lying flat on the pad. As the lid came down the sharp end went through my glove and into my thumb. Taking the gloves off, I encouraged the wound to bleed, went quickly to the sink and washed it copiously with water. It looked such a trivial injury, yet I was only too well aware of the potential implications.'

The patient and his family were well-known to us. The father was a part-time shoemaker with a drink problem, two wives and a large number of children. He had tuberculosis, and the others were suffering from malnutrition. All had been tested for AIDS in the past with negative results, with the exception of one of the little girls. This didn't make sense. For a child of this age to be HIV-positive, the source had to be the mother, who had shown up negative. The mother and children were tested again. This time the results were positive. The boy died a few days later.

Now Roger had to be tested. The first blood sample, taken by Debbie, showed he was HIV-negative at the time of the injury. Then it was necessary to wait three months before taking a further test, to see if he had been infected through the needle. In the meantime every sniffle, ache or pain was a source of worry. Thankfully, the second test came back negative too. However, he admitted, 'The sense of relief was not as great as it should be. I'm negative now, but what about the next accident with a needle, or the one after that?'

Roger subsequently went through the dilemma that many other overseas workers have experienced in the face of danger. Fight or flight? He couldn't escape the problem, for all around were AIDS patients.

One morning, walking to the hospital, he saw a group of women sitting on the ground under the shade of a tree. Their tell-tale wailing meant only one thing: someone had died during the night. The notes of a patient were lying on the floor just inside his office door. They had been put there by one of the night nurses. Roger picked them up, sat at the desk and started to read them.

She was only a young woman. Single, but with a child a few months old. She had first come to the hospital complaining of a cough, weight loss and severe diarrhoea. She certainly looked as if she had lost weight, she was so emaciated. An X-ray showed that one side of her chest was full of fluid. Treatment was given, but her condition deteriorated. The previous day Roger had tried draining two litres of fluid off the chest. Obviously it had made no difference. A blood test confirmed she had AIDS. A few days later the child also died.

Another patient, who was pregnant, had such severe vaginal warts, caused through AIDS, that she couldn't deliver normally. She was given a Caesarean section. The baby survived and seemed fine. Though he was feeding, he did not grow at the normal rate, became sickly and ultimately died. Of AIDS.

'At times, I don't feel I can cope with the pressure,' said Roger. 'It must be similar to the predicament you were in during the war. But I think this is worse because this enemy is hidden, and therefore seems more sinister.'

But he did cope, eventually declaring, 'Though I wanted to leave and find a safer occupation, I realised two things: I can't just run away, and no job is without hazards. I could go home and who knows? An accident or unexpected illness could take me. Life is not something we can hold securely in our own hands. What did Jesus say? "For whosoever will save his life shall lose it: but whosoever will lose his life for my sake, the same shall save it"' (Luke 9:24, KJV).

Meanwhile my own health was fine. However, my temperament was adjusting to some of the non-medical matters a Sister in Charge has to cope with. Like pilfering. Ten litres of diesel oil and two door frames were reported missing from the hospital storeroom. A close check was kept, and smaller items also started to disappear.

On Elim Secondary School's sports day, the people handling the refreshments ran out of sugar. Roger was around, and offered to go and fetch some from a small shop run by Mai Malvira. The sugar was kept in large containers, not pre-packed as in Western supermarkets. After weighing, his purchase was put into a plastic bag. Roger soon realised this was one of our sterilisation bags. Evidence!

Mai Malvira also had a job in the hospital. She was brought into my office for questioning, but denied theft. The explanation was that the bags were being thrown away. I was not satisfied, and suspended her pending further enquiries. The police had to be called in and an officer gave a talk to all the staff. It looked as if Mai Malvira was guilty, but I didn't want her sent to prison. We opted for a disciplinary warning, after which she was reinstated, but she failed to turn up for work. I believe this may have been due to embarrassment. Pastor Satuku mentioned the matter in church, to clear the air, so everyone knew the true story of what had been going on.

A happier occasion was the visit of President Mugabe to the hospital on 24th October 1990. He seemed impressed and stayed for several hours. It was very hot—another of those days when we were eagerly awaiting the rains. Due to the heat and old age, an elderly lady died while he was there. But we managed to steer him away and avoided the distress of letting him see the body being carried out. I believe she died of a heart attack. She only came in with an abscess on her face.

I was ill again in March and April of 1991, with fevers, aches and pains and then a rash—typical of the type common with typhoid fever. Roger started me on the treatment for typhoid and then I was driven in to Harare for further investigations. No conclusive diagnosis was made. If I had been tested for AIDS at that time, I wonder, would the result have been positive?

Next I had a strange rash on my thighs and abdomen in December. The doctor in Harare was most interested, but had no idea what it could be. He prescribed steroids, which seemed to help. As soon as the course was finished the rash came back with a vengeance—just for one day—before completely disappearing. I never had it again.

On 19th February 1992 I was helping in the operating theatre. A man had mangled his hand in a grinding machine and attempts were being made to tidy up his fingers. It was a long and delicate procedure. I started feeling hungry and then dizzy. The room was spinning round. I grabbed at one corner of the operating table in order to stay upright. No one seemed to notice me.

Suddenly, gripped by agonising abdominal pain, I cried out, 'Help! Go and fetch Debbie!' One of the African nurses ran out to fetch her. With my head on the table alongside the patient, I made sure he was kept asleep by shooting anaesthetic into a vein every time he moved. By the time Debbie arrived on the scene I was on the floor. But the patient was still asleep. I was escorted home, took some painkillers, and went to bed. When I woke up I felt fine, as if nothing had happened.

In the days that followed, the problems with my throat and chest developed. The next part of my story you know—the diagnosis of AIDS, my journey back to England and hospitalisation have already been told in

Chapter 1. But that is not the end. As a PWA (person with AIDS) I am not just sitting around waiting to die. The following pages show I am living a full life, as actively as possible. And God is leading me into a new understanding of himself and his ways.

9

After living abroad for so many years, I sometimes feel the world has passed me by. Whenever I have spent time at home in the past it has been hard to make many lasting friendships, because I would soon be off to another part of the world. In the same way, I have allowed myself to become distant from my family—to be less involved in their lives than if I had been in England throughout the last twenty years. Some members of the family have been mentioned in previous chapters. Now is the time for you to hear more, as I rediscover them.

My parents Victor and Violet have been happily married for over fifty years. They had six children. Unfortunately the first baby died. Some brothers and sisters are like peas in a pod. The five Baths have varying temperaments and have all done different things.

Roy is the eldest. He used to help in Dad's shop and now works for the Post Office. He lives with his family in Swindon. Jacquie, his wife, is a kind of extra daughter to Mum and Dad, and a sister to me. Originally from Jersey, she was adopted by another branch of the family and is technically my cousin. As a child she was always round at our house, playing with the rest of us. Roy and Jacquie have two grown-up children, Kevin and Mandi.

I came next, born on 17th April 1950. In some churches a child's first communion or confirmation service might be a cause for celebration. The Pentecostal way records when an individual makes their own decision to become a follower of Jesus. I became a Christian at the age of eight, which is quite young, but not that unusual. I received the baptism of the Holy Spirit at the age of sixteen.

Pearl was born after me. She has a husband called Trevor and daughters Charlotte and Geraldine. They all live in Salisbury. When Charlotte realised my second term of service in Zimbabwe was among AIDS patients, she organised a collection service for rubber gloves from local hospitals and clinics. She was just thirteen years of age at the time.

My brother Tim and his wife Yvonne live in Swindon with young Kristian and James. When Tim is not working as a chef, he and Yvonne can often be found in Russia. As part of Messianic Testimony to the Jews they deliver humanitarian aid to needy families in an orphanage, intensive care unit, and the Russian National Centre For Children With AIDS. Their work also involves sharing the gospel with Messianic believers. Russia is currently experiencing a dramatic spiritual awakening, and the Jewish community is no exception to this. Since the collapse of Communism, literally thousands of Jewish people have come to acknowledge Jesus as their Messiah.

Keith, my youngest brother, is married to Debbie. They are about to begin a family of their own. In the meantime he has several hundred four-legged babies to care for. Keith is a shepherd on Salisbury Plain. It's a rugged life, being out in all weathers.

Quite often Keith will come over for lunch. We have so much in common, sometimes our conversation horrifies Mum and Dad, especially if we are all enjoying a meal together. With Keith a shepherd and myself a midwife, the discussion frequently turns to the similarities between the birth of a baby and a lamb. It is natural for us to compare our different experiences, but either Mum or Dad will interject with, 'Please, you two! Not while we are eating.'

On one such occasion Keith was worried about an old ewe, who might have to be put down. She had developed a bad infection. Though Keith would ensure that any treatment was carried out humanely, he was upset at the thought of losing a member of the flock. I am surprised at the compassion and concern Keith shows for the sheep. If one of the lambs is sick or weakly, his wife is given the job of nursing it back to health in their kitchen.

I hate the idea of pain being experienced by any living thing. But for human beings it can come in many forms; physical, mental and emotional; persecution and rejection. It can act as a purifying process. It can be a benefit, remoulding a person and giving new strengths.

A student social worker called Emma has visited me on a regular basis. She is a tremendous girl who, as a sufferer of cerebral palsy, has already overcome many hurdles to reach her current role. I wonder whether she would have been so keen to succeed if she were not fighting a disability.

Some Christians, mostly those who do not understand how AIDS is spread, have made hurtful comments to me. They spit out accusations like, 'You must think we're naïve to say you caught it at work. From an affair, more like.' As a result I have started to feel a closeness to the Virgin Mary. Her pregnancy, while engaged to Joseph, must have prompted winks and nudges from the gossips. If she had told all and sundry that God was the father of her baby, she would either have been locked up for being insane, or stoned to death for blasphemy. Instead she not only bore all the taunts silently and with dignity, but was also able to utter a wonderful hymn of praise, which is nowadays known as the Magnificat. It has become something I recite often in my private times with God:

> My soul glorifies the Lord and my spirit rejoices in God my Saviour, for he has been mindful of the humble state of his servant. From now on all generations will call me blessed, for the Mighty One has done great things for me—holy is his name. His mercy extends to those who fear him, from generation to generation. He has performed mighty deeds with his arm; he has scattered those who are proud in their inmost thoughts. He has brought down rulers from their thrones but has lifted up the humble. He has filled the hungry with good things but has sent the rich away empty. He has helped his servant Israel, remembering to be merciful to Abraham and his descendants for ever, even as he said to our fathers (Luke 1:46–55).

To keep things in perspective, I've encountered little negative reaction to my condition. However, I have been guilty of a few wrong attitudes myself towards other people. When visiting Southampton for hospital appointments, I have to report to the Genito-Urinary Clinic. This is more commonly known as the STD (Sexually Transmitted Diseases), VD or Special Clinic. It is embarrassing to sit in the waiting room there, never having had a sexual relationship. And it is not easy to have an unbiased attitude towards other patients. I have tried to reason the matter through, saying to myself that the other people are there because they are sick, and who am I to judge how they became ill?

I had an interesting discussion with Jacquie along these lines, which led to some radical conclusions:

1. I shouldn't ask or even think about how another person contracted AIDS, unless I am prepared to submit myself to their prejudices and suppositions about me.

2. As Jesus was the friend of sinners, he might have shown more sympathy and compassion than I have so far towards other AIDS sufferers. He might have shown more willingness to be identified with them.

3. How can I be more like him? When asked how I came to be infected, perhaps I should just say, 'Through my work in Africa,' and not go into long explanations about being an innocent victim.

I have had five or six boyfriends. The physical side of the relationships has never progressed as far as the sexual act. Even the naughtiest thing I ever did along these lines is really quite innocent. While training to be a nurse in Poole, a mutual attraction developed between myself and a patient. I used to draw the curtains around his bed so we could kiss and cuddle. That was as far as it went. The sheets always stayed between us. It was most unprofessional conduct and I was lucky not to be caught and thrown off the course. Nothing like that ever happened again.

Over the years it has been hard to see those close to me finding partners and getting married, while I am still single. Now I have AIDS there is even less possibility of ever having a family of my own. I often feel I would love to be married; to have someone to care for me and someone to care for. Then I look around and see so many marriages in shambles. Perhaps I am better off as I am.

Reaching out to make new friends at this stage in my life is such an effort. But I know I must do it, and have joined Salisbury AIDS Support Group. I made the first move, contacting the co-ordinator David Penney, and arranging to meet at his office. We chatted at length. He is a very understanding person, concerned for the downtrodden of our society. Among the many posters on the wall of his office, I noticed one which read something like, 'No one ever died of AIDS by caring.' I could accept what the poster was saying, but pointed out that's exactly the way I contracted AIDS. The poster has since been removed.

Occasionally I come across faces from the past. A girl who was one of my Sunday school pupils in the 1970s was recently baptised at Elim Salisbury Church. Although contact had been maintained with people there, she had faltered in her faith since childhood, until she heard me speak at a luncheon. Before being baptised, she walked to the microphone and said, 'Joy's done so much with her life. But over the last twenty years, what have I done with mine? Very little. This moment symbolises a new start for me.' It was touching to think that my testimony could have such an effect on someone else's life.

Since January 1993 I have undertaken a number of speaking engagements at churches and conferences. They have all been valuable in helping people to understand what it is like to have AIDS. I generally feel I should address the problem of why Christians suffer. This is a vast subject, but starting to explore it has helped me, and I trust it has helped others too.

I believe suffering is not a licence for self-pity, but a chance for the sufferer to teach and encourage others. Shakespeare said that all the world is a stage. The audience can see us playing our part well, or badly. If all is well, they receive something positive to take to their hearts and take home. If all they see is hatred and bitterness the message of the scriptwriter is lost; the time spent at the theatre wasted.

There are Christians who believe healing is waiting just around the corner for everyone who is sick. They see the absence of healing as proof of a lack of faith in the promises of God. Their reasoning is based on certain passages of Scripture, for example Matthew 7:7–11 and 21:18–22, which seem to indicate human beings can obtain anything they ask. Then there are the many instances of Jesus healing people miraculously. I do not doubt the abilities of the Almighty, but in becoming a Christian I became a follower of Jesus. He suffered an agonising death, and if that means I have to do the same for some reason, I must say, 'Thy will be done.'

Three passages of Scripture have been particularly helpful to me. Sometimes, as I read these aloud to congregations, I find it hard to control my emotions. The words seem so powerful and simple:

First, 2 Corinthians 1:3–11, especially:

> . . . the God of all comfort, who comforts us in all our troubles, so that we can comfort those in any trouble with the comfort we ourselves have received from God . . . Indeed . . . we felt the sentence of death. But this happened that we might not rely on ourselves but on God, who raises the dead (vv 3b–4, 9).

Second, 2 Corinthians 4, especially:

> We are hard pressed on every side, but not crushed; perplexed, but not in despair; persecuted, but not abandoned; struck down, but not destroyed. We always carry around in our body the death of Jesus, so that the life of Jesus may also be revealed in our body . . . Though outwardly we are wasting away, yet inwardly we are being renewed day by day. For our light and momentary troubles are achieving for us an eternal glory that far outweighs them all. So we fix our eyes not on what is seen, but on what is unseen. For what is seen is temporary, but what is unseen is eternal (vv 8–10, 16b–18).

Third, Philippians 1:20–21, especially:

> . . . Christ will be exalted in my body, whether by life or by death (v 20b).

These passages have also helped me to cope with a worsening state of health. Though I am certainly not living every day in the hope that it is my last, I am looking forward to an afterlife I am certain exists.

My parents' house benefits from the famous view of Salisbury Cathedral across green fields. One of my favourite pleasures on a fine day is to walk the rural lanes there, gazing at the water meadows from Britford Bridge. One Saturday I was out walking when I passed a house where a man was working on his car. Parts and tools were all over the pavement and I tripped on them. It wasn't that I was day dreaming. I just could not see them or the ground beneath my feet. For some months I had been experiencing bad headaches and blurred vision around the lower edges of my eyes. Now some of my peripheral sight had gone.

Dr Wilmot in Southampton said a virus named cytomegalo was responsible. If untreated, it could take my sight completely. He arranged for the fitting of a Hickman Line. This is a tube attached to a main vein near my heart, with the outer end about two inches long, sticking through my chest. With a bit of adjustment it remains hidden by my clothing. Five days a week an anti-viral solution called Ganciclovir is slowly injected through the Hickman Line. The process takes about two hours and I can administer the treatment myself. It seems to have helped stem the sight loss, but the headaches are still with me.

Normally supplies of Ganciclovir arrive at home by a special delivery service. But on one occasion a mix-up over the prescription meant I had to collect it from a hospital pharmacy in Southampton. Also waiting for drugs there was an African girl. She looked familiar, but I could not think whether we had met before. Then I remembered a conversation with a nurse which took place before I was allowed home to Salisbury.

'Joy, I don't know whether I should ask you this, but there's an African lady in the next isolation cubicle with the same problem as you, who doesn't know how she's going to cope. Would you have a chat with her?'

'Yes, I will. I'd like to meet someone else with my condition.'

'And you might be able to speak in her mother tongue?'

'Probably not. There are loads of different tribal languages. But I might be able to help in some way.'

I tried to keep my promise, but I was receiving a lot of visitors every day. Each time I was alone, she had someone at her bedside. By the time we were both free she was being discharged and her husband was taking her away. But here she was again, at the pharmacy. I seized the opportunity to introduce myself.

She was feeling much better, and had found a part-time job. We exchanged addresses and in due course she and her husband came to visit me. It was a great encouragement for both of us. And it was comforting for her to chat with another person who had lived in Africa.

I was also put in touch with another PWA, a young man in a more serious condition. I went to see him on several occasions. He was painfully thin, and had several infections, which eventually killed him.

Since coming back to England I have been able to attend two Elim conferences. At the most recent, intense headaches meant it was only possible to go to a few sessions. One of these was a children's meeting where I gave a talk. Afterwards they prayed for me, particularly a young coloured lad called Gideon. He showed real faith and it made me quite tearful. A younger child had a prophecy from the Lord: 'Jesus wants us to know he loves us all very much. And Joy, he's proud of you.' I was more blessed by the words of these little ones than by the carefully prepared lectures of seasoned preachers.

Work, church services, speaking engagements and conferences. You may be wondering whether I ever relax and have a good time. Members of some religions believe everything on earth has been put here for us to enjoy. To some extent Pentecostals agree with that, but in practice they try to avoid anything which might be termed worldly or extravagant. In doing so we have become separated from some of life's more innocuous pastimes. For most of us, going to church is the highlight of the week. We really enjoy it—possibly because the services are so lively and uplifting. The rest of the time we are too busy adhering to the Protestant work ethic to notice all the good things in the world around us. We have largely forgotten how to have a good time—at least I had until I was forced into early retirement.

Recently I have been on more outings and holidays, have had more fun, than ever before. I treasure memories of walking along a cliff path on Guernsey, followed by delicious crab sandwiches at Vazon beach; joining in a sing-song with others in the crowd during a carnival procession; sunlight sparkling on a calm sea, as I took a ferry to the Isle of Wight; just sitting at home watching the *Last Night of the Proms* on television with a box of chocolates on my knee.

I went to London's Oxford Street and travelled on an open-top bus to see the Christmas lights. What an experience! It was dark and freezing cold, but I was wrapped up warmly. There was a wonderful atmosphere, with the Salvation Army band playing carols and the beauty of the street lights and window displays. The trip was something I had wanted to do for years, but never managed it before. Then there was the joy of having the family together—all twenty-six of us—on Christmas Day.

I have found happiness in all kinds of everyday pursuits. The key is to relax, stop rushing from one task to the next worrying about the future, and enjoy what the present provides. Try it sometime. I only wish I had earlier.

During my enforced stay in England I have had a lot of time to reflect upon my life. I think it was while I was in India that I had a conversation with a fellow missionary about the right time to go home. My condition is fuddling my mind and I am unable to remember who the person was, but their words have remained with me. It was said that a missionary can get to the stage where Asia, Africa or some other continent is so much a part of them they cannot do without it. That's when it is time to return home. I now think that maybe I had reached that stage with Zimbabwe.

10

Fairly recently, while reading part of the Sermon on the Mount (Matthew 6:31–34), I was struck by the words of Jesus, 'Do not worry about your life.' I am sure he did not mean we should not plan and prepare for the future as best we can. He did mean we should not be full of anxiety. He goes on to say, 'Therefore do not worry about tomorrow, for tomorrow will worry about itself. Each day has enough trouble of its own' (v 34).

What really impressed me about this teaching of Jesus was the air of authority with which it was delivered. He was not giving out advice, but commands. And how right he was to place emphasis on this matter. It is pointless to waste our lives sitting around fretting about things which may never happen. On the other hand, if we knew the trials we had to face in life beforehand, we would probably give up on every aspect before reaching adulthood.

Two letters posted from Nyanga just before Christmas 1992 shocked and saddened me. First Roger Drew wrote that Peter Griffiths was seriously ill. Then Peter himself told me that the outlook was bleak. Yet the start of his troubles seemed so small and insignificant.

At the beginning of November Peter was reading aloud, as a prelude to giving one of his regular Tuesday evening Bible studies to a large group of people. He could not pronounce some of the words properly. No one except Brenda seemed to notice, and he put the problem down to being overtired, plus the fact that the passage of Scripture—from Genesis—contained some tricky Hebrew names.

The next day Peter's speech was slurred from time to time. He wrote: 'I rang Debbie Murphree, the GP, and arranged an appointment. Foolishly ignoring her advice to get someone to drive me to her rooms, I drove myself. She found a slight weakness on the left side of the face, which could indicate I had suffered a minor stroke. After the examination she immediately arranged for me to see a consultant, Terry French, the following day.'

A CAT scan arranged through the consultant showed that a part of Peter's brain, about the size of a golf ball, appeared to have died. At least that was the first impression. When he saw the pictures Terry French commented, 'That's a pretty impressive infarct of the brain!'

An infarct is an area of dead tissue caused by interruption to the blood supply. This would probably fit in with the supposition that Peter had survived a stroke.

Peter had wisely asked his son Stephen to take him to this appointment. From Roger Drew's letter came the news, 'Stephen and his wife Anna had been due to fly to Mozambique that day, to begin work with the Leprosy Mission. Thank goodness they were delayed due to a shortage of aviation fuel. Peter had an epileptic fit in the car as they drove away, just outside the grounds of Terry French's office.'

The normally tranquil atmosphere of the consulting rooms was shattered by their return. Stephen, who is a doctor himself, helped to put up a drip and administered diazepam, a sedative, through a vein. An ambulance quickly arrived and Peter was taken to Parirenyatwa, a large hospital in Harare. Stephen was quite distraught by the sight of his stricken father. Of the fit, Peter said, 'Fully conscious throughout, I thought I was dying. I yielded myself to the Lord, thinking he was taking me home to heaven.'

Several more fits happened that day before Peter's condition calmed down. A neurosurgeon, Mr Auchterlonie, said surgical intervention would not be necessary. About a fortnight later, while Peter was still in hospital, he took a sudden turn for the worse, losing strength on his left side. A second CAT scan was done and this time the picture was enhanced by injecting dye. Terry French and Mr Auchterlonie realised that what appeared to be dead tissue was in fact a tumour.

Wrote Peter, 'I was transferred to the Avenues Clinic where Mr Auchterlonie operates from—literally! He did a biopsy of my brain. There was a two-day, agonisingly long wait for the results. They showed the tumour was malignant, and ought to be removed without delay. I signed the consent form for the operation.'

The apparent strokes were caused by the tumour bleeding into itself, swelling rapidly and putting pressure on certain areas of Peter's brain, resulting in paralysis down the left side of the body.

Roger saw him before surgery, and reported, 'Physically, he was worse. The left arm and leg were now also affected. Naturally, Peter was apprehensive about the operation. But he was doing his best to crack jokes—bad ones as usual—and responded well to a comment made by one of the nurses.'

She had come to wish him luck. Peter replied, 'I don't believe in luck. I believe in God. If this is my time to die, I'm ready.'

The operation went well, and the surgeon managed to remove all of the tumour. Peter recalled, 'The following days were just a blur. As a nurse, you'll realise how I must have looked, with tubes going into me and coming out of me in all sorts of places. And I was sedated up to the eyeballs. But in my confusion, God was revealing new depths of his love and graciousness. As I lay in that bed I marvelled at how God loves this world, and me as a part of it, and at how he deals with us in wonderful ways we do not deserve. I reflected with awe on the scene in Gethsemane, when Jesus saw the horror of his approaching death and said, "Father, if you are willing, take this cup from me; yet not my will, but yours be done" (Luke 22:42). Discharged from hospital, I am now at home. Mr Auchterlonie is setting up programmes of radiotherapy and chemotherapy at Parirenyatwa. The battle continues and I ask for your prayers.'

Strength, co-ordination and clear speech were returning to Peter. Progress was slow, but he was hopeful for the future. I was not so sure. It was no surprise when a third letter came through the letterbox a couple of months later, containing bad news. Peter wrote, 'I have been told there is no cure in medical science for my condition. The sort of tumour I had invariably returns. Radiotherapy simply controls the growth rate for a time, and may give me a little longer to live. So, you and I are in the same boat. Tell me how you cope.'

I knew Peter must be pretty low to send out such a plea, so I was on the telephone to him straight away. He didn't seem too bad, but admitted to struggling with despondency on waking each morning, due to thinking about the future.

He said, 'Depression fades somewhat as I become active and involved in the affairs of the day.'

We decided he was suffering from an over-fertile imagination. He was prone to thinking about what would happen if he became disabled to the point of being like a vegetable.

'Thoughts like that are not allowed!' I chided. 'Remember the Briens' prayer?'

'Lord, help us to live in the light of eternity. There are

times when I feel I'm beginning to learn to stand where God stands, and to take an overhead view of what's happening in this brief span of time. Then, in my disabled state, I stumble over some object, or falter in a simple everyday task like a clumsy child, and come back down to earth. It's very hard to accept. I've always been such an active person.'

For the next six months Peter and I supported each other with letters and telephone calls. In a way it was comforting to know that such an old and trusted friend was going through the same kinds of thoughts and feelings as myself. At one stage I had half a plan put together to fly over to Zimbabwe and visit Peter, Brenda and others. It was an impossible dream which never materialised. My health would not have stood up to such vigorous travelling.

The tumour began to grow again, and by late summer Peter's condition was deteriorating. Susie Sanguinetti, a friend who worked for the BBC World Service, began typing his letters to me. 'I am now walking around slowly and once more speaking with some slurring of my speech,' I read. The next paragraphs let me know in no uncertain terms that he would not be with us much longer.

> I have given the family instructions for my funeral. I want to be buried, rather than stick to the European practice here of cremation. This is because my African friends find cremation a difficult idea. The preacher and leader of the service will be Dr Ken Jenkins, but Pious Munembe and Ephraim Satuku should also speak. They are so close to me and risked their lives for me during the war here.
>
> I want two hymns which have special meaning for me. 'Amazing Grace', because I have become more amazed than ever that God should treat me, and the whole world, with grace we are not worthy to receive. And '*Ungatora Hako Pasi*', which Brenda and I had at our wedding. The Shona roughly translates, 'You can take the world and all its joys. We for our

part will take Jesus and all he offers. His grace is overwhelming and sufficient for all.'

Now I must go and take an aspirin gargle—a small thing you and I do in common! Your loving and very tired friend and colleague, Peter.

Those were the last words he ever wrote to me and I treasure them, like a person might hold on to an old pair of worn out shoes. Brian Edwards rang me on the morning of Tuesday 10th October to say that Peter had died at 9pm the previous evening. The funeral would be on the following Friday in Mutare, conducted according to Peter's wishes. A memorial service was held in Swansea on 6th November. I was able to attend, with Mum and Dad. A good number came and it was an incredibly moving occasion. Afterwards Peter's mother gave me a long and tearful hug.

We stayed overnight in Wales and travelled back the following day. I drove all the way there and most of the way home. As we left the M4 at Chippenham I moved over to let Dad take the wheel. Exhausted, I was also acutely aware of my failing eyesight. It was getting to the point where it was no longer safe for me to be in control of a car. Just as Peter's treatment had only delayed the growth in his brain, I feared the Ganciclovir was fighting a losing battle within my own body.

Over the next weeks my health began to deteriorate. I carried on with the treatment, but suffered dreadful migraines whenever I was up and about. So I stayed in bed, sleeping for most of the time. When I did manage to stagger about on my feet I experienced weird feelings of weightlessness, as if I were floating above the ground. These symptoms could have been due to stress and grief; reactions to Peter's death. They disappeared when I was presented with a wonderful surprise.

Early one morning the doorbell rang and my parents

instructed me to answer it. David Butcher and his wife were on the front step, both grinning from ear to ear.

'We picked up something special for you at Heathrow at the crack of dawn,' he said. 'Come and have a look in our car.'

I was intrigued as they led me through the door and a few paces up the drive. Someone was sitting on the back seat of the car. I couldn't see who until I looked inside.

'Jeya! I never thought it would be you out here.'

'I never thought to leave India—though I did visit Singapore last year—but you, my friend, are worth coming all this way to visit!'

We both wept happy tears and held each other for several minutes. Until David suggested the house would provide a more comfortable place to sit.

Jeya stayed about a week and was a real tonic. We are similar people, in spirit rather than looks, capable of holding deep conversations and discussions. I interviewed her as part of a Sunday service at Salisbury Elim Church and she shamed me by offering this lovely tribute to our friendship: 'God brings many people in our lives to be a blessing for us. God brought Joy into my life to give me joy.'

When it was time for Jeya to leave England I made the journey to Heathrow with her, escorted by Mike and Elisabeth Sherwood. He is an Elim pastor based in Essex, who formerly worked for Brian Edwards in Elim International Missions. Mike's face beamed as Jeya told how the GEMS has grown at an amazing rate in recent years. The work has expanded from Bihar to surrounding states and into the neighbouring country of Nepal.

Our parting was difficult. Jeya is an intuitive girl, and she knew this would be our last contact this side of heaven. It was a lovely day and I was not allowing any thoughts of an untimely death to invade my mind. I just thought this was another of those occasions when her emotional Indian temperament took over. After checking in her luggage, Jeya clung on to me, sobbing. Elisabeth gave her a handkerchief with which to wipe her wet face.

Jeya took a couple of deep breaths and quietened down a little. As we approached the barrier she clasped my hands in her own and said, 'God has told me that he is going to give you a special blessing in glory.'

She meant I would be rewarded in heaven for experiencing a short life. A sense of calm came over the four of us as Jeya walked off to the plane. Mike, Elisabeth and I gave each other a knowing glance. It was a look that said, 'Who knows? Perhaps she's right.'

From then on, my attitude to death changed. I could no longer carry a vague acceptance that for me life would be brief. I knew I would die young. And within me came a firm, almost tangible excitement at the thought of meeting my Lord Jesus face to face.

Hundreds of daffodils line the roads of Salisbury each spring. They were there like a welcoming committee when I came home in 1992 and provided a vibrant sign of hope to me the following year. How uplifting to see their glorious yellow show again as I was taken out for a treat to mark the second anniversary of my return from Africa. The doctors had not expected me to live this long. Now Mum, Dad, Pearl and I were lunching in a restaurant, celebrating the fact that an extra twenty-four months of life had been granted.

Pearl had never been supportive of my desire to work overseas. Nor had she experienced the Christian faith in the same way as other members of the family. When I contracted AIDS she became bitter and resentful. There were arguments and tears. The gap of understanding between my sister and the rest of us widened into a great chasm.

My mother is a level-headed person—an ordinary housewife who is not prone to vivid imaginings. During the meal she announced, 'I had a dream—or rather a vision. It was so real I know it came from God. It means I mustn't worry about what happens to Joy.' Dad and I were told about this earlier in the day. Pearl looked up from her plate astonished, fork poised halfway to her mouth.

Mum's eyes, always big and bright, grew even larger as she described what she had seen. 'I was in the most lovely garden with Joy. There were flowers everywhere. We walked by a great mass of roses. Red, white, yellow, peach, pink—every colour you could think of. Each bloom was perfect. Their combined scent was overpowering. Jesus was there and he came and stood between us. He held one of our hands in each of his own, so we were one either side of him. Then everything went black.'

We all carried on eating for a few moments. Sniffing back a couple of tears, Dad dabbed at the edges of his mouth with a napkin. Mum leaned over to Pearl earnestly. 'I think Joy will be taken before long. But it's all right, because I've been given a glimpse of where she's going.'

'Yes, I believe you have,' replied Pearl thoughtfully. She accepted the statement without question, knowing our mother could never concoct such a story.

After this, Pearl began to visit us more often. She came to stay at the house, to be with me while our parents took a holiday together. We became much closer and even prayed together during that week, which meant a great deal to me.

It was necessary to have someone around, for my eyesight was becoming steadily worse. I first noticed the upper and side vision in the right eye had gone one Sunday morning in church. Pentecostals go in for a lot of hand raising: it is a Jewish custom St Paul helped to perpetuate by saying he wanted 'men everywhere to lift up holy hands in prayer' (1 Timothy 2:8). So we can often be found with our arms held high. On this occasion I realised I could not see my right arm at all.

In addition, breathing difficulties were starting to return; I quickly became breathless when walking. And oral thrush had developed. Time for a visit to the hospital in Southampton. Too weak to walk from one department to another, I was pushed around in a wheelchair. It was humiliating to think how my freedom was slowly being taken away. All the time I was there, my constant prayer was, 'Lord, please preserve the sight in my left eye.'

Bad eyesight or not, I could see that the ward I was in had not been cleaned properly for some time. With the aid of a magnifying glass I wrote out a formal complaint. It took some time. The domestic supervisor and her superior appeared by my bedside.

'Only the bed table is done by the cleaners. The cleaning of the TV table, locker tops and mirror shelf is not our job,' I was told.

'Oh, so who cleans those surfaces then?' I asked.

'The nurses!'

The pair bustled off, giving the impression that a fuss was being made about nothing. However, the next day, when I came back from having an X-ray, my area was spotlessly clean. I have no idea which of the staff was responsible.

The balance between domestic and ward responsibilities is an age-old problem encountered at most hospitals. Unfortunately dust and grime hold germs, and someone has to wipe them away or else patients may be at risk to infections.

There was good news about my eyes. While the doctors admitted there was an advancement of sight loss, they said the virus was now under control. No further deterioration should occur. Apparently the PCP left a weakness in the lungs. An aromatic treatment of menthol and eucalyptus was prescribed for my chest. And I was given something for the thrush before being allowed home.

It wasn't long before the bad headaches returned. This time, though they resembled migraine, they were much worse. The pain extended down the sides of the face to the gums, and was particularly bad around the eyes. With the headaches came nausea, resulting in a loss of appetite. Then the sight in my right eye began to flicker, like a light being switched off and on.

One morning I awoke from sleep with my head on the left, with the good eye closed against the pillow. I could see nothing on the right. I was completely blind on that side. The medics had been mistaken; the virus was not beaten. Terrified at the thought of going absolutely blind, my mind filled up with all kinds of imaginary scenarios. If my parents died, would other members of the family be able to care for me? What if I had an accident, or started a fire while they were at work?

Suddenly, I understood how Peter Griffiths must have felt when his thoughts took off in all directions. Once more I prayed for God to keep my left eye safe and in good working order.

11

Summer clothes were packed away and out came the warm sweaters and trousers. How I hate having to change my wardrobe twice a year. I miss the African sunshine. This time, as I carefully folded up my pretty cotton dresses, I wondered if they would ever be needed again.

Once more I was admitted to hospital in Southampton. The retina of my right eye had become detached, and that was the reason for the blindness. Nothing could be done to restore the lost sight. There was more concern about my breathing difficulties and the fact that I had lost weight. A cough had developed too. I was put in an isolation ward.

As I lay in bed, receiving frequent attention from the nurses, I remembered some of the advice I used to hand out to carers.

'Sit the patient up, raising the head on pillows to assist breathing. People tend to panic when they can't breathe properly, and that makes them even more wheezy. During panic attacks, stay by their side, encouraging them to stay calm and take regular breaths.' Now people were doing the same things for me. I couldn't help but smile.

Far more visitors came than I could cope with. Sometimes I had to ask them to wait outside while I took a nap. Debbie Brown came over on furlough and it was a real tonic to see her. We joked that I was so weak I should be in geriatrics. It was good to learn that since my departure from the Mission hospital at Katerere, new regulations had been made to protect staff against HIV infection.

'Nowadays we go into the operating theatre dressed for a moon walk!' she told me.

'Well, I'm sure it's much safer that way. If only I'd been more careful, perhaps . . .' Unexpected feelings of sadness and anger washed over me.

'You mustn't blame yourself.'

'Yes, I must. I was in charge—of myself and the rest of you. This is the price I've had to pay for my negligence.' I started to cry. Tears of bereavement for the loss of my own life.

It was an entirely appropriate moment for a doctor to arrive and tell me I would soon be discharged. Apart from making my last months as comfortable as possible with the help of drugs like morphine, there was little more that could be done to combat the HIV in my body. I was being sent home to die.

My story had previously attracted the attention of the Christian press. On release from hospital, Mum and Dad contacted a secular news agency. Journalists began queuing at the front door; photos appeared in the national press; interviews were given for radio and television. What a way to become famous!

Hundreds of cards, letters and presents arrived from all over the globe. So many, it was not possible to reply to everyone who sent them. From closer to home came a request from the new Bishop of Salisbury, the Right Reverend Dr David Stancliffe. He wanted to know if I was strong enough to receive him as a visitor. I said 'yes'.

Before he arrived, I indulged in a few musings as to what he might be like. Perhaps he would wear special robes and speak perfect English in a sing-song voice. Would he expect me to call him 'My Lord Bishop' I wondered? All these ideas were quickly dispelled when he arrived in a businesslike suit, with clerical shirt and collar, and announced, 'Hello, I'm David.'

We sat down together. He was easy to talk to, and listened with interest as I told him something of my calling and work in Zimbabwe. He seemed genuinely moved.

'When a bishop is appointed, it is customary for groups of colleagues and parishes to give various items of episcopal insignia as gifts. If it were not so, it would be difficult to make ends meet. Members of the Liturgical Commission—of which I recently became Chairman—said they would like to present me with something.'

He had already been given a fine bishop's ring by the Bishop of Portsmouth, but said he would very much like to have a smaller and more discreet one which could be worn when not on official business.

'A reasonably simple gold band was found, like a man's wedding ring. The hallmark on the inside showed the year I was ordained to the priesthood. It was inscribed in Carolingian script *IN TE DOMINE SPERAVI*: "In thee, O Lord, have I put my trust." This is a quotation from the last verse of the *TE DEUM*, which forms part of the Anglican Order for Morning Prayer.' Leaning forward, he took the ring he was talking about from his own hand, to show me the words. I could just about see them with my good eye.

He explained, 'I chose this motto because it is all too easy for bishops as well as other people to start putting their confidence into management exercises, or new schemes, or the institutional church, or whatever, instead of in God.'

I nodded, adding that he could include medicine in that list.

'Joy, there is a sense in which a bishop is married to his diocese, taking on its concerns, its parishes and people. When I was consecrated I received special responsibility for outcasts, the poor and those who cannot help themselves. I have little to share with you, except my care for the poor. You have sacrificed your life for their sake. I want to be identified with that sacrificial quality; that giving of oneself regardless of the cost. So I want to give you this ring. It will be a link between us. Will you accept it?'

I had already been impressed that a Church of England bishop was taking an interest in the trials of a Pentecostal. Now a lump came to my throat as I took the precious possession from him.

'I will be proud to wear it, and encouraged by the message it contains.' He seemed quite humbled. A look of understanding went between us; a bond of acknowledgement had been formed that we were both servants of the same God.

I have worn the ring every day since. It is a little large for my slender fingers. Mum wound some embroidery silk around the inside edge, to ensure it does not slip off.

At the beginning of December each year there is World AIDS Day. In 1994 I used my newsworthy status to obtain more publicity for this event. Some of the stories used the angle that I would be dead by Christmas. Spurred on by the challenge to prove the media wrong, I not only lived through the festive season, but also enjoyed it. I even put on a little weight in the process.

I did miss out on the carol services, though. It is not possible for me to attend church any longer. I am too weak, and can only walk a few steps around the house before becoming tired. Instead, Mum stays home with me on a Sunday and we worship together. Sometimes other members of the family or friends come over and join us. These are times I really enjoy. I still have my voice, and can sing the old hymns and modern choruses as loud as I like.

Early in the New Year someone interviewed me and said

the number of AIDS cases worldwide had risen to more than a million. My reply was that it can only get higher. As yet there is no vaccine, no cure. I was also informed that four other nurses have contracted the disease in the same way as myself: victims of their patients.

As Britain moved into a winter of torrential rain, with people being stranded in dreadful floods, one of my worst nightmares came true. The sight in my left eye failed. I am now totally blind. It is so hard to accept. But even this disability has brought unexpected blessings. My hearing is so acute I can hear the smallest sounds. I love to have the bedroom window open and listen to the birdsong. I never really noticed they were there before. It is a mystery to me how such tiny creatures can make such lovely music. I will not be able to see the golden daffodils this year. However, when flowers arrive for me, I can take pleasure in gently running my fingers over the petals. They are so soft and fleshy in a way nothing else is.

The pains in my head and feelings of sickness would be constant and unbearable now if it were not for the morphine intake, which has been increased. It turns me into a giggling girl, but it works. My appetite is extremely poor. I eat less and less. I have become all skin and bone. Every little movement hurts.

Lying still in bed, with nothing else to distract me, I feel God is close all day and night. He is here when the District and Macmillan nurses come to give treatment; when Jacquie relieves Mum or Dad at my bedside; as Roy is heard cutting the back lawn. I pray out loud, 'Lord send someone to make me comfortable.' It feels as if my bones are on the outside of my skin.

Good Friday 1995. The family have church around my bed. It is lovely. I am so full of praise, my arms go up in the air and I shout, 'Hallelujah!' I know I will not live to experience my birthday next week. I do not care. I will be in a better place.

Drifting in and out of consciousness now. Dreams and visions of heaven. Or are they real? I hear Dad say, 'She's going.' Then all my pain disappears as I leave my earthly body behind. My soul is released into the next world. I leave behind me no offspring. This book is my legacy for all those who are children of this age of AIDS.

Note

The risk of HIV infection from social contact or normal day-to-day activity is effectively non-existent. However, health care workers are regularly exposed to risk through accidents with needles, operating instruments or through blood contamination of their own wounds. Despite this, the risk of transfer of HIV from an infected person is still far less than for, say, hepatitis B. For example, an injury from an HIV contaminated needle will result in infection only one time in 200 accidents, compared to 1 in 5 from hepatitis B. Joy may have been accidentally exposed to HIV many times as she worked in an area where the number of carriers is very high. Health care workers can greatly reduce risk of infection by following normal infection control guidelines.

Dr Patrick Dixon MA MBBS
Founder of ACET (Aids Care Education and Training)

Epilogue

Eunice Joy Bath died in the early evening of Easter Saturday, 15th April 1995, two days before her forty-fifth birthday.

On 26th April her funeral service was held in her own beloved Elim Church in Salisbury, attended by almost 300 people: family, church friends, nursing colleagues, school and college associates. Interment followed in Salisbury Cemetery.

Three weeks later a celebration of thanksgiving for Joy's life took place in Salisbury's Playhouse Theatre, attended by over 450 people from all over the British Isles and Africa. Appreciations were given by Mrs P. Rycroft—immediate past Mayor of Salisbury; Doctor R. Drew, Sister D. Brown and the Revd P. Munembe—all from the Elim Mission at Katerere in Zimbabwe; the Revds W. Lewis and B. Edwards—both of Elim Executive Council, and G. Ladlow and M. Hathaway of Salisbury Elim Church.

It was Joy's wish that the inscription on the headstone of her grave should read: 'Greater love has no one than this, that he lay down his life for his friends' (John 15:13).

The Bath family cannot personally reply to all correspondence. Enquiries about Joy, overseas work undertaken by the Elim Pentecostal Church, or questions about the Christian faith, should be directed to:

Elim International Missions
P.O. Box 38
Cheltenham
Gloucestershire
GL50 3HN
England